Leading Change through Transformational School Leadership

Dimensions of Leadership and Institutional Success: Exploring Connections and Partnerships

Series Editor: Ellen H. Reames

The *Dimensions of Leadership and Institutional Success* series focuses on issues related to leadership preparation and development and how leadership fosters success in a wide variety of contexts such as K-12 schools, universities, business, health professions and professional schools. Sub-themes include scholarly treatment and practical implications of the role of collaborations, partnerships and ways of connecting to build relationships and leadership capacity.

OTHER TITLES IN THE SERIES

Educational Leadership Program Coordinators: Partnership Creators Through Social Connectedness

Navigating the Ubiquitous, Misunderstood, and Evolving Role of the Educational Leadership Program Coordinator in Higher Education

Partnerships for Leadership Preparation and Development: Facilitators, Barriers and Models for Change

Leading Change through Transformational School Leadership

Edited by

Jeffrey Glanz
Michlalah Jerusalem College, Israel

United Kingdom – North America – Japan
India – Malaysia – China

Emerald Publishing Limited
Emerald Publishing, Floor 5, Northspring, 21-23 Wellington Street, Leeds LS1 4DL

First edition 2025

Copyright © 2025 by Emerald Publishing Limited.
All rights of reproduction in any form reserved.

Cover photo: courtesy of Drazen_/iStock.com

Reprints and permissions service
Contact: www.copyright.com

No part of this book may be reproduced, stored in a retrieval system, transmitted in any form or by any means electronic, mechanical, photocopying, recording or otherwise without either the prior written permission of the publisher or a licence permitting restricted copying issued in the UK by The Copyright Licensing Agency and in the USA by The Copyright Clearance Center. Any opinions expressed in the chapters are those of the authors. Whilst Emerald makes every effort to ensure the quality and accuracy of its content, Emerald makes no representation implied or otherwise, as to the chapters' suitability and application and disclaims any warranties, express or implied, to their use.

British Library Cataloguing in Publication Data
A catalogue record for this book is available from the British Library

ISBN: 978-1-83708-983-3 (Print hardback)
ISBN: 978-1-83708-985-7 (Print paperback)
ISBN: 978-1-83708-982-6 (Ebook)
ISBN: 978-1-83708-984-0 (EPub)

Typeset by TNQ Tech
Cover design by TNQ Tech

CONTENTS

About the Editor vii

About the Contributors ix

About the Series Editor xiii

Editor's Introduction xv

1 Democratic Leadership for School Change 1
   Stephen P. Gordon

2 Creating Change Through Developing a Growth Mindset in a Large High School 21
   Lee Westberry

3 Leading Change to Improve the Professional Development of Israeli Teachers 37
   Michael Reichel, Shmuel Shenhav, Daniel Chester, & Shoshana Karlinsky

4 Needed—Coherent System Transformation to Build Capacity and Leverage Learning During System Innovation 59
   Sally J. Zepeda, Grant M. Rivera, Beza Tefera Muzein, & Kathryn Polley

5 Leading Change Through Instructional Leadership 75
   Haim Shaked

6 Transforming Teaching Quality With Intelligent Accountability 89
   Helen M. Hazi

7 Shifting Paradigms in Principal Leadership: Entrepreneurial
  Middle Leader Amidst Transformational Change 105
  Chun Sing Maxwell Ho

8 Transforming Schools Through Reflective Dialogue..................... 125
  Rachel D. Solis

9 "Learning Loss" and Other Misguided Narratives for
  Impeding Educational Change 143
  Ira Bogotch & Eleanor Su-Keene

ABOUT THE EDITOR

Jeffrey Glanz is a Professor and Head of the MEd program in Leadership and Management in Educational Systems at Michlalah Jerusalem College. He held the Silverstein Endowed Chair in Professional Ethics and Values and was a tenured professor of Education and Administration at the Azrieli Graduate School of Yeshiva University. He was Dean of Graduate Studies and Chair of Education at Wagner College in Staten Island, New York. He was executive assistant to the president at Kean University, and at Kean, he was named Graduate Teacher of the Year by the Student Graduate Association. He was also the recipient of the Presidential Award for Outstanding Scholarship. He was a teacher and school administrator in New York City for 20 years. Prof. Glanz has authored, co-authored, edited, and co-edited twenty-six (26) books on various educational topics, the most recent with Rowman & Littlefield Publishers, *Creating a Culture of Excellence: A School Leader's Guide to Best Practices in Teaching, Curriculum, Professional Development, Supervision, and Evaluation*. yosglanz@gmail.com; www.jeffreyglanz.com

ABOUT THE CONTRIBUTORS

Ira Bogotch is a Professor of Educational Leadership at Florida Atlantic University. Currently, he is co-editing both the *Second Edition of the Springer International Handbook of Educational Leadership and Social (In)justice: Critical Perspectives*, and the *Second Edition of Education, Immigration, and Migration: Policy, Leadership, and Praxis for a Changing World*. ibogotch@fau.edu - FAU | Dr. Ira Bogotch's Research on Educational Leadership and Social Justice

Daniel Chester is a research lecturer in the Department of Management and Organization of Education Systems at Jerusalem College. He managed an educational team for about 10 years. Currently, he is responsible for professionally preparing male teachers in Haredi institutions, part of the Israeli Ministry of Education. Research areas include sources of power for school principals, school management in emergency situations, authority relations of school principals, acceptance of authority, and challenges and experiences of new school principals in Haredi society. ddchdd@gmail.com

Stephen P. Gordon is a Distinguished Professor Emeritus at Texas State University. He received his doctorate in supervision from the University of Georgia and received the Association for Supervision and Curriculum Development's national award for the outstanding dissertation in supervision. At Texas State University, Dr. Gordon taught courses in educational leadership and was Co-director and later Director of the National Center for School Improvement. He has published over 70 articles and chapters and authored, co-authored, or edited 19 books. His most recent texts are *Developing Successful Schools: A Holistic Approach* (2022) and *Supervision and Instructional Leadership: A Developmental Approach* (2024), co-authored with Carl Glickman, Jovita Ross-Gordon, and Rachel Solis. Dr. Gordon has been honored with the University of Georgia College of Education's Lifetime Achievement Distinguished Alumni Award. SteveGordon@txstate.edu

Helen M. Hazi is a Professor Emerita of Educational Leadership at West Virginia University and was a student of the East Coast version of clinical supervision represented by Morris Cogan and Noreen B. Garman. She has been a teacher, a supervisor of curriculum and instruction, and an expert witness. Helen is a Council of Professors of Instructional Supervision member and a founder of the AERA SIG: Supervision and Instructional Leadership. She writes about legal issues that have consequences for supervision and teacher evaluation in books and journals such as *Journal of Curriculum & Supervision*, *Journal of Educational Supervision*, *Journal of Staff Development*, *Teachers and Teaching: Theory and Practice*, and *Educational Policy Analysis Archives*. She is exploring judgment and feedback's role in teacher evaluation and instructional improvement. hmhazi@verizon.net; https://helen-hazi.faculty.wvu.edu/home

Chun Sing Maxwell Ho is an Assistant Professor of the Department of Education Policy and Leadership and Associate Co-Director of the Academy for Education Development and Innovation at the Education University of Hong Kong. Dr. Ho has been invited to hold school leader training programs for primary and secondary schools in Hong Kong. He was awarded the 2021 Emerald Young Researcher Award and the 2023 Michael Fullan Emerging Scholar Award in recognition of his contribution to research and practice and its impact on Hong Kong's schools. hocs@eduhk.hk

Shoshana Karlinsky is a graduate of Michlala Jerusalem College, where she earned her Master's Degree in Educational Leadership. Her thesis focused on teacher professional development (PD) and the role played by principals in fostering positive PD. She has been teaching English in high school for 24 years, and she is an English coordinator who offers PD. Over the past 6 years, she has worked as an English Counselor in the Israeli Ministry of Education, developing and implementing varied English pedagogical programs in high schools. shoshkarl@gmail.com

Beza Tefera Muzein is a second-year PhD student in Education Administration and Policy and a Graduate Research Assistant at the Mary Frances Early College of Education at the University of Georgia. With experience as an Assistant Registrar, Beza has a strong background in educational administration and was a teacher. She is passionate about breaking down barriers hindering students' success and is particularly interested in Supervision, Classroom Walkthrough Observation, Professional Development and Coaching. bezimu.tef1@gmail.com; beza.muzein@uga.edu

Kathryn Polley is a PhD candidate in the Department of Educational Theory and Practice, and she is a Research Assistant in Educational Administration and Policy at the Mary Frances Early College of Education at the University of Georgia. A former music teacher and lifelong teacher educator, she studies issues surrounding K-12 teachers' sense of belonging, well-being, and professional learning. kathryn.polley@uga.edu; kathryngpolley@gmail.com

Michael Reichel is a Lecturer in the Leadership and Management in Educational Systems at Michlalah Jerusalem College. He was a school administrator in elementary and middle schools for over 20 years in the USA and was the Principal of the Chorev Elementary School for boys in Jerusalem, Israel. His research interests include management leadership, theories in educational administration, bridging theory with practice in educational administration programs, and recruitment strategies for hiring qualified principals. He recently co-edited *Principal Recruitment and Retention: Best Practices* with Rowman & Littlefield Publishers. rmreichel@hotmail.com

Grant M. Rivera has been the proud superintendent of Marietta City Schools (MCS) since 2016, overseeing 13 schools, around 8,900 students, and 1,200 staff. A career educator, he has experience as a principal, teacher, and coach. Dr. Rivera believes learning to read and write is one of life's most fundamental achievements and a leading indicator of future success. He leads MCS in setting a new standard for what it means to invest in literacy education. With degrees from Northwestern University and the University of Alabama, he's actively involved in education organizations and is committed to raising awareness and funds for pediatric cancer. grivera@marietta-city.k12.ga.us

Haim Shaked is the President of Hemdat College of Education, Sdot Negev, Israel. As a scholar-practitioner with almost twenty years of experience as a school principal, Professor Shaked's research focuses on principalship, particularly instructional leadership and system thinking in school leadership. He has published more than sixty refereed research articles and book chapters and edited and authored books on these topics. In 2022, his book *New Explorations for Instructional Leaders: How Principals Can Promote Teaching and Learning Effectively* was published by Rowman & Littlefield. haim.shaked@hemdat.ac.il; https://haimshaked.com/

Shmuel Shenhav is the Head of the Graduate School of Education at Michlalah Jerusalem College, in Bayit Vegan, Jerusalem, Israel, Head of the Avney Rosha Program for the professional development of school leaders in the Israel Ministry of Education, and Head of the National-Religious Center for Leadership in Israel. He served as a school principal for many years. He is a national speaker on issues related to educational leadership and has published in journals such as the *International Journal of Educational Reform* and the *Journal of Practitioner Research*. shenhav@huji.ac.il

Rachel D. Solis is an educational coach and consultant who has served in schools as a teacher, assistant principal, director of human resources, and director of faculty professional development. She co-authored the 11th edition of *SuperVision and Instructional Leadership: A Developmental Approach* (2024) and has authored and co-authored articles on assisting teachers' reflective inquiry, supervising action research, supporting formal and informal teacher leadership, and integrating multiple learning formats to assist professional growth. Dr. Solis's research interests and focus areas as a consultant center on teacher learning and development, reflective dialogue, and practitioner inquiry for school improvement. She is a reviewer for several educational journals and a recipient of the Blumberg/Pajak Scholar Award. rachel.delane@gmail.com

Eleanor Su-Keene is an Assistant Professor in the Teaching, Learning, and Culture Department at Texas A&M University in Texas, USA. As a former K-12 educator, she is interested in school leadership and improvement, particularly at the intersections of health, social justice, and sustainability. Her more recent work conceptualizes the impacts of stress and mental health on principal and teacher workforce sustainability and re-conceptualizations of social justice leadership through humanizing practices. esukeene@tamu.edu; https://directory.education.tamu.edu/view/esukeene

Lee Westberry is an Associate Professor of Educational Leadership in the Zucker Family School of Education at The Citadel Military College in Charleston, S.C. She is also the Program Coordinator for the Division of Ed Leadership and the Director of the Anita Zucker Institute for Entrepreneurial Educational Leadership Center of Excellence. Before working with the Citadel, Dr. Westberry worked as a school administrator at the middle school, high school, and district levels. Recent publications include *Putting the Pieces Together: A Systems Approach to School Leadership*, *The Final Piece: A Systems Approach to School Leadership*, and *The Virtual Principal: The Many Facets of the Demanding Role*. lwestber@citadel.edu

Sally J. Zepeda is a Professor at the University of Georgia in the Department of Lifelong Education, Administration, and Policy in the Mary Frances Early College of Education. She teaches courses related to instructional supervision, teacher and leader evaluation, and professional learning. She has written over 80 journal articles and book chapters and authored, coauthored, or edited over 40 books, including the 5th edition of *Instructional Supervision: Applying Tools and Concepts* translated into Turkish, and the highly acclaimed 3rd edition of *Professional Development: What Works* (with Routledge). Dr. Zepeda also co-edited the *Wiley Handbook on Educational Supervision*. Dr. Zepeda's co-authored book, *Leading School Culture Through Teacher Voice and Agency*, is being translated into Korean by Hakjisa Publisher, Inc. Dr. Zepeda works with many school systems in the US and internationally to support teacher and leader development. Through a collaborative partnership, she works with the Marietta City Schools, assessing the transfer of professional learning and the science of reading. szepeda@uga.edu

ABOUT THE SERIES EDITOR

Ellen H. Reames is a Professor of Educational Leadership at Auburn University. Prior to coming to Auburn University, Ellen spent thirty years as a K-12 teacher and administrator. She researches educational leadership program design and enjoys exploring innovative ideas that can improve the lives of K-12 school administrators and teachers. Her current focus includes the influence of positive psychology and mentoring for principal well-being and developing educational leadership preparation program partnerships. Dr. Reames has authored five books: *The Art and Science of Mentoring* (2021); *Rural Turnaround Leadership Development: The Power of Partnerships* (2018); *Partnerships for Leadership Preparation and Development: Facilitators, Barriers and Models for Change* (2020); *Navigating the Ubiquitous, Misunderstood, and Evolving Role of the Educational Leadership Program Coordinator in Higher Education* (2023); and *Educational Leadership Program Coordinators: Partnership Creators Through Social Connectedness* (2024).

EDITOR'S INTRODUCTION

As Editor, I am excited to introduce a book in which I am serving as the editor: *Leading Change through Transformational School Leadership*. We are living through tumultuous times, given the unpredictable technological advances, the instability of world politics, the ever-increasing economic disparities worldwide, and the ubiquitous social and cultural upheavals dominating the news through social media. Amid these global social, political, economic, and cultural transformations, education and schooling remain constants for hope, prosperity, and resilience. Schooling, in particular, and education, in general, have been stable institutional and organizational structures serving students of all ages globally. Schools aren't merely reactive to outside pressures but are, ideally, proactive institutions aiming to forge a better society that provides the requisite knowledge, skills, and ethical dispositions necessary to function in an ever-changing 21st-century milieu. Schools serve to provide high-quality instruction as well as to reinforce common values of goodness, equity, and justice for all.

Consequently, schools, although stable forces, must change to meet the challenging needs of 21st-century living. School leaders, in particular, are responsible for creating ways to improve the educational experience. Whether it's adapting the curriculum to meet societal exigencies, creating new programs to support student learning, advancing the education of teachers, providing greater access to parental involvement, forging connections with the surrounding communities, and much more, schools must remain at the forefront of educational change.

This edited volume provides insights into the change process as school leaders grapple with many demanding challenges. Chapters in this volume draw from the real world of practice, highlighting attempts to navigate an ever-increasing complex, diverse environment and grappling with internal and external vicissitudes that inevitably challenge a school leader's convictions and intestinal fortitude. Because problems are more intractable today, school leaders have relied on several theories of leadership to guide their work in schools. Transformational school leadership theory provides foundational guidance but also draws from other literature bases concerning teaching, learning, teacher leadership, and systems thinking (e.g., improvement science), which are formative.

Each chapter in *Leading Change Through Transformational School Leadership* draws on an expansive leadership literature base to address different yet important change initiatives. The chapters address the challenges and opportunities to affect positive school changes that benefit student learning academically, emotionally, and socially.

Much of the published literature on school change is dated and, or lacks a theoretical grounding in the change literature. Many works offer suggestions without concretizing the change initiatives within the confines of real-world practices. *Leading Change Through Transformational School Leadership* is unique for several reasons: (1) It avoids the aforementioned deficiencies; (2) It provides insights into the change process that are grounded in extant theories about change while, at the same time, highlighting real-life efforts to implement important reform initiatives in school settings; and (3) provides, at the end of each chapter, brief case studies with thoughtful follow-up questions for readers to reflect on the process of school change.

This work is intended for all kinds of school leaders (superintendents and related supporting staff, principals, APs, deans, chairs, etc.) at all school-based levels, i.e., elementary, middle, high school, college, and university. The book can be used in principal preparation programs at the college and university levels at the master's and doctoral levels. It will also appeal to policymakers. The cases in this book are particularly useful in PD opportunities to discuss and learn about implementing change realistically.

Each chapter follows a basic template format, beginning with Pre-focus Guiding Questions to stimulate thought about the major ideas discussed. An Introduction sets the tone for the chapter, providing theoretical background or extant research to support the ideas presented in the chapter. Coming right before a Summary, practical implications of the ideas presented in each chapter provide ideas and tools to actualize school change. A realistic case study with follow-up reflective questions engages the reader to think about the ideas or concepts of each chapter.

* * * * * * * * * * *

Allow me to say a few words about each of the contributions.

In Chapter 1, Stephen P. Gordon introduces the concept of deep democracy, which considers all community members to be equal, worthy of respect, and entitled to participate in decisions that will affect them. Deep democracy also recognizes that community members are interdependent and thus have a responsibility to work together for the common good. A focus on deep democracy, it is argued, promotes continuous school improvement, improves student achievement, and prepares students for citizenship in a democratic society. However, due to the traditional organizational structure of schools and other political and social factors, the movement toward deep democracy is challenging. Transformational leadership is needed to facilitate the transition from conventional to democratic schools. The transformational school leader assists members of the school community in developing a democratic vision, challenges and supports members as they move toward that vision, facilitates changes in the school organization and culture, and helps the school community to apply democracy to the core functions of the school: teaching and learning. Prof. Gordon goes beyond a call for advocacy by providing educational leaders with practical guidelines to democratize schooling.

In Chapter 2, Professor Westberry focuses on creating a singular school culture of continuous growth at the high school level. She posits that change is never easy, and cultural change can be the hardest to create. High school content area teachers often cluster together and isolate themselves from others in the building. Thus, the challenge of creating cohesion and a growth mindset among all faculty requires a transformational leader. The chapter presents an actual attempt to alter the culture of a large high school, from maintaining the status quo to developing a growth mindset among all faculty. This change was aimed to increase improvements in student achievement and increase collective self-efficacy among staff members. Challenges faced, mistakes, and lessons learned are shared in this chapter. Specific examples are given in the areas of creating a shared vision, building a culture of collaboration, and empowering teachers to lead – all tenets of transformational leadership.

Chapter 3 contributors, Drs. Reichel and Shenhav, along with Research Lecturer Daniel Chester and a recent master's graduate student Shoshana Karlinsky, report on a mixed-methods study analyzing the results of a questionnaire distributed to 217 school leaders (teachers and principals) to assess the state of teacher professional development [PD]. Interviews were also conducted with 20 school principals. PD, in many schools, is episodic, often administered in a top-down fashion initiated without meaningful input by teachers, among other problems. The study conducted by the chapter authors reflects several intractable issues in offering effective PD. The discussion focuses on the importance of transformational and instructional leadership to make PD more effective on several levels. Concrete suggestions for doing so are proffered.

In Chapter 4, Professor Zepeda and colleagues examine the lessons learned as a school district in the United States pressed forward to reform literacy instruction in grades 1–3 by moving to the Science of Reading. The complexities of transformational change on a district level are meticulously addressed. Coherence between the district and school levels underlying this system-wide change across eight schools is emphasized as critical to the change process. In addition, the attention to coherence in policies, practices, and processes illustrates that when school districts innovate, they can build capacity and leverage learning for adults. This chapter offers a unique contribution with insights into large-scale system transformation.

In Chapter 5, Professor Shaked explores the conceptual framework of instructional leadership within the broader context of transformational school leadership, highlighting its critical role in facilitating change in schools. Not too long ago, instructional leadership was not viewed as a principal's primary or at least a very important responsibility. More and more school systems now, though not enough, have paid closer attention to the importance of instructional leadership. Instructional leaders primarily aim to transform teaching and learning in alignment with the school's mission, evaluate instruction and programs, and facilitate curriculum and professional development by creating professional learning communities to promote student learning and achievement. The chapter focuses on the four main elements of instructional leadership: instructional vision, instructional program, instructional climate, and teacher development. Each element is addressed in detail, drawing from extant literature and research and drawing practical implications.

In Chapter 6, Professor Hazi tackles several taken-for-granted notions about teacher evaluation, which she decries as a failure. Instead, she introduces the concept of "intelligent accountability," which represents a system that can transform teaching and learning, encourage participatory leadership, and promote a professional learning community, all aspects of transformational leadership. She presents this concept as a way to think about helping teachers transform and account for their practice through self-reflection and evaluation. The role of team teaching, peer observation, self-evaluation, and evidence literacy are explored within a system of intelligent accountability and as a way for principals to transform and improve individuals and groups of teachers. She highlights a school known as Corbett Prep, an independent day school where teachers team to plan, teach, and assess instruction. Her work provides guidance to educational leaders who are dissatisfied with traditional practices of teacher evaluation with promising practices for change.

Chun Sing Maxwell Ho, in Chapter 7, discusses middle school leaders as instrumental in actualizing transformational leadership through entrepreneurial action. These leaders create a vision, but the vision is actually challenging, given various organizational constraints and challenges. The paper focuses on the efforts of a middle school principal to convert visionary principles into concrete, actionable outcomes that nurture environments ripe for middle leaders and school improvement. The study offers a wealth of insights for transformational leadership at the middle school level in transforming otherwise traditional organizational policies and practices into actionable strategies and thoughtful reflections on nurturing a culture of innovation and adaptability. By dissecting the experiences of middle leaders who have successfully navigated the transition from conceptual frameworks to tangible educational outcomes, the chapter provides strategies to equip school leaders with the knowledge to empower their teams, advocate for resourceful problem-solving, and champion a collaborative approach to leadership.

In Chapter 8, Rachel Solis asserts that reflective dialogue facilitated effectively by educational leaders can transform perspectives and practices to improve schools. While reflection supports us to understand where we are and where we want to be, dialogue allows us to deprivatize beliefs and collectively work to actualize change. Leadership for school change through reflective dialogue entails fostering "deep conversations" centered around educational beliefs and the relationship between those beliefs and the school's day-to-day practices. Reflective dialogue, above all, challenges individual and institutional assumptions, explores diverse perspectives, fosters critical thinking, and leads to informed and intentional decision-making that enhances teaching and outcomes for students. Dr. Solis, an educational coach and consultant working with classroom teachers, departmental teams, and school leaders to foster reflective dialogue, shares examples and insights from the literature and practice to demonstrate the power of reflective dialogue to empower and encourage shared leadership and align the connection between the specifics of school practices and student learning.

The book ends with a most critical review of the change process offered by Professors Bogotch and Su-Keene. We end the book with this chapter because it challenges us to think deeply and critically about school-district change. Change, they argue, is ever-present and inevitable. Yet the tools and strategies we have utilized to affect meaningful change are neither sustained nor institutionalized as described in traditional change theories. Drawing upon the consequences of the COVID pandemic that led to "learning loss," they posit that an opportunity for real change was possible to thwart educational state and national imposed mandates for standardized testing and compliance to other innate measures. They draw upon transformational leadership literature to promote true emancipation, democracy, equity, and justice. The chapter contributors challenge readers to break through taken-for-granted notions of change by introducing the notions of narrative and disruptive leadership that, in the words of Maxine Greene, urges educators to "find an aperture in the wall of what is taken for granted; to pierce the webs of obscurity; to see and then to choose." Drs. Bogotch and Su-Keene end the chapter with a realistic case focusing on educational change beyond traditional conceptualizations of educational leadership. *Leading Change Through Transformational School Leadership* thus ends with no easy solutions but much to consider.

* * * * * * * * * *

Change is both difficult and necessary. It's difficult because people and organizations prefer stability and tradition. It's necessary because technological, social, and cultural forces demand new ways of looking at and doing things. The change process is complex. I would be remiss if I didn't cite the work of the person who has probably given us the most significant insight into the change process: Michael Fullan. His work is formative, inspirational, and practical.

The contributors to this volume have given us diverse insights into the change process from a transformational leadership perspective. Transformational leadership focuses on organizational change through visionary and charismatic leadership aimed at improving schools. Transformational leaders articulate an ethical and moral vision for their work and seek to engage educational stakeholders in efforts to redesign the organization. The contributors to *Leading Change Through Transformational School Leadership* echo such a vision. Theories have been addressed, and practical strategies have been presented. It's up to our readers to think, reflect, and act upon the information we present.

Finally, to encourage readers to reflect on the issues presented, I have created a WhatsApp Leadership group to continue the conversation. I welcome you to join and participate by posing questions, offering suggestions, and reacting to others in an effort to share and grow together as a community of learners and concerned educational leaders.

Follow this link to join my WhatsApp group: https://chat.whatsapp.com/CLW9fX2nPsxAw1Q5mACzmf.

We also urge you to contact the contributors of this volume to further the conversation. Emails are provided for each contributor.

Thank you for your continued success, professionally and personally.

Jeffrey Glanz
June 2025

CHAPTER 1

DEMOCRATIC LEADERSHIP FOR SCHOOL CHANGE

Stephen P. Gordon
Texas State University, USA

ABSTRACT

In Chapter 1, Professor Stephen P. Gordon introduces the concept of deep democracy, which considers all community members to be equal, worthy of respect, and entitled to participate in decisions that will affect them. Deep democracy also recognizes that community members are interdependent and thus have a responsibility to work together for the common good. A focus on deep democracy, it is argued, promotes continuous school improvement, improves student achievement, and prepares students for citizenship in a democratic society. However, due to the traditional organizational structure of schools and other political and social factors, the movement toward deep democracy is challenging. Transformational leadership is needed to facilitate the transition from conventional to democratic schools. The transformational school leader assists members of the school community in developing a democratic vision, challenges and supports members as they move toward that vision, facilitates changes in the school organization and culture, and helps the school community to apply democracy to the core functions of the school: teaching and learning. Prof. Gordon goes beyond a call for advocacy by providing educational leaders with practical guidelines to democratize schooling.

Keywords: Democratic leadership; transforming schools; democratic school communities; non-traditional school organizations; democratizing schooling

---

Prefocus Guiding Questions

- *What are the primary characteristics of a deep democracy?*
- *What are the primary attributes of a democratic school principal?*
- *What are some ways each of the following can provide democratic school leadership: (a) teachers, (b) students, (c) students' families, (d) other community members?*

INTRODUCTION

A critical purpose of public schools in a democratic society is to prepare students for democratic participation in that society. Students learn democracy best in democratic schools, which require democratic leadership. This chapter describes deep democracy, what it looks like in schools, and the challenges of introducing it to a school.

The school principal is key to the facilitation of democracy in a school, and the dispositions, skills, and activities of the democratic school leader are described in this chapter. The relationship between democratic and transformational leadership is discussed. A variety of structures and processes for implementing democratic school leadership are reviewed. Although the principal's leadership is critical, in a democratic school community all stakeholders—teachers, students, students' families, and other members of the community who are committed to the school—become democratic leaders, and this chapter examines how each of these stakeholder groups can practice democratic leadership. There are many benefits of democratic leadership and democratic schools, which are summarized in the latter part of the chapter.

DEMOCRATIC LEADERSHIP AND DEMOCRATIC SCHOOLS

Deep Democracy

One way to understand "deep democracy" is to compare it to "thin democracy." Thin democracy includes such elements as personal freedom, individual privacy, the right to vote, and majority rule. Thin democracy clearly is not a bad thing, but it is insufficient. A fully democratic society embraces deep democracy, as described by Dewey (1916):

> A democracy is more than a form of government; it is primarily a mode of associated living, of joint communicated experience. The extension in space

of the number of individuals who participate in an interest so that each has to refer [their] own action to that of others, and to consider the action of others to give point and direction to [their] own, is equivalent to the breaking down of those barriers of class, race, and national territory which kept [individuals] from perceiving the full import of their activity. (p. 87)

Literature on deep democracy (Dewey, 1916; Furman & Starratt, 2005; Green, 1999; James, 2010; Kadiver et al., 2020; Ralls, 2019; Woods, 2021; Young, 2000) describes its beliefs, goals, and decision-making process. Those committed to deep democracy believe in the worth and dignity of all people and the interdependence of community members. They also embrace freedom as "a mental attitude rather than external unconstraint of movements" (Dewey, 1916, p. 305). The goals of deep democracy are the growth and development of all individuals, mutually supportive relationships, and the common good.

Decision-making in a deep democracy is inclusive. Members treat each other as equals and share power. At the same time, each member is expected to participate in the decision-making process and accept their share of responsibility for decisions that promote the common good. Decision-making in a deep democracy involves free inquiry and open communication, with diverse opinions welcome. Participants respect one another throughout the decision-making process; they listen to and consider each other's ideas, critique those ideas when appropriate, negotiate differences, and work toward consensus.

Deep Democracy in Schools

Deep democracy in schools means that everyone, including each adult and each student, is valued and respected. A common purpose unites all members of the school community. The common purpose differs from school to school but always reflects a commitment to democratic leadership, democratic teaching, and democratic learning, preparing students to contribute to a democratic society. Jenlink and Jenlink (2008) remind us that "learning communities defined by democratic practices are communities that include rather than exclude, that create knowledge rather than assume that others produce all knowledge, and that expect controversy and conflict to be part of the educative process" (p. 314).

Stakeholder activities in a deeply democratic school tend to merge: the principal, teachers, students, and students' families all engage in leadership, teaching, and learning. All participate in open inquiry, critical reflection, and dialogue within and across the different groups that make up the school community. Examples of democratic activities all stakeholders (including students) can engage in include school governance, inquiry on how to improve curriculum, teaching, learning, and student assessment, increasing equity at the classroom, school, and community level, and service to others in the school and outside community.

How do stakeholders know they have achieved deep democracy? Gordon and Boone (2014) propose three criteria: inclusion, integration, and internalization. A school meets the *inclusion* criterion when all stakeholders in the school community are involved in the democratic process. *Integration* means that democracy is embedded in all critical aspects of classroom and school life. *Internalization* means that democracy becomes synonymous with the school's culture: "democracy becomes an assumption, a habitual way of dealing with people and situations, a way of life" (p. 52). For schools that have not yet met these criteria, the important thing is continuous growth toward deep democracy.

The Promise and Challenges of Introducing Deep Democracy in Schools

In a school practicing deep democracy, "school members share power, authority, and critical decisions; examine and act upon issues of equity; and consider serving others both within and outside the school" (Williams et al., 2009, p. 468). Deep democracy in schools leads to school improvement, teacher growth, and improved student learning. Democratic schools prepare students to be better citizens and to help sustain a democratic society (Glickman et al., 2024). Later in this chapter, a full review of the positive effects of democratic school leadership is provided, but, for now, a less positive reality needs to be discussed. Despite the promise of deep democracy, most schools are not authentic democracies. This reality calls for an analysis of the challenges to introducing deep democracy in schools and how democratic school leadership can navigate those challenges.

One challenge is what Alderson (2004) refers to as myths about democracy in schools. Some of these myths include beliefs that deep democracy is a wonderful idea but not realistic, that only adults can participate in democracy, that the primary purpose of schools is to socialize students, and that adults must control schools. Another myth discussed by Alderson is that students are best prepared for citizenship by learning ideas and facts *about* democracy rather than learning *in* and *through* democracy.

External pressure on schools is another challenge to democratic schools. For example, Klinker (2006) argues that in the US, "the business community plus state and federal governments are now major players in education. This involvement often chips away at the foundation of democracy, its grass roots" (p. 52). External challenges may also come from district administrators or groups from the local community opposed to democratic schools.

The previous history of the school may be a challenge to deep democracy if that history is one of top-down leadership. If teachers are used to taking directives from the principal and giving directives to students, and families are used to receiving directives from the school, it will be difficult (but not impossible) to transition to a democratic school. Also, if different groups focus on their rights and needs at the expense of other groups, it will be difficult for the school community to embrace collective action for the common good. A related problem is the lack of equity for historically marginalized groups, as deep democracy cannot flourish without equitable treatment of all groups.

How do school leaders committed to democracy navigate the challenges described above? A beginning point is to engage all stakeholders—educators, students, families, and other community members involved with the school—in dialogue about what deep democracy looks like and the positive effects of such democracy. Various groups that make up the school community need to develop skills to engage in democracy, and such skills can be taught through professional development, family education programs, and the school curriculum. Regarding the barrier of inequity, Uy et al. (2024) suggest the following:

> Inclusive decision-making processes must actively address issues of privilege, voice and representation to ensure that the needs and perspectives of all stakeholders are adequately considered (Sykes et al., 2012). This necessitates creating structures and mechanisms that promote equitable access to decision-making opportunities and facilitate the inclusion of marginalized voices. (p. 182)

For stakeholders not used to or comfortable with democratic decision-making, Glickman and Mette (2020) recommend an incremental approach. Formal leaders initially ask stakeholders to choose from options presented to them but, over time, ask those stakeholders to accept full participation in the decision-making process.

Dispositions, Skills, and Activities of the Democratic School Principal

Democracy does not naturally emerge in the conventional school; it needs to be facilitated, and the school principal is the most likely party to provide that facilitation. Several dispositions distinguish the democratic school principal. The principal cares for all members of the school community and thus is committed to listening to those members, meeting their needs, and empowering them (Larsen, 2024). The leader respects and trusts others and expects others to trust them (Harris & Chapman, 2002).

The principal is guided by a set of ethical values, including a commitment to equity, the desire to serve others, and political courage, and communicates those values to others (Gerstl-Pepin & Aiken, 2009).

The democratic school principal also displays various skills necessary to facilitate democracy. Skills for engaging in open dialogue and building trust with stakeholders are essential (Harris & Chapman, 2002). Facilitating democratic collaboration within and across groups requires the principal to possess collaborative skills, including active listening, conflict resolution, creative problem-solving, and consensus-building (Uy et al., 2024). Moreover, Woods (2021) describes "politically adaptive" skills needed when there is resistance to democracy. These skills include those needed to protect members of the school community from external powers opposed to democracy, negotiate differences between the principal's values and the values of other stakeholders, respond to power issues between stakeholder groups, and mediate between instrumental (e.g., student test performance) and substantive (e.g., meaningful learning) goals.

The democratic school principal is both a facilitator and active participant in democratic decision-making. As Glickman and Mette (2020) explain, "in the democratic approach, a leader with formal authority is allowed (and expected) to participate in the group decision-making process, but hierarchy is flattened and formal authority does not determine decisions" (p. 68). Early in developing a democratic school, a critical activity of the principal is working with stakeholders to develop a school vision. The vision should both be created through the democratic process and guide future efforts to develop the school as a deep democracy. Once the school vision has been adopted, the principal has the responsibility of leadership consistent with that vision (Larsen, 2024).

Another essential activity of the democratic principal is to foster a school culture that encourages and rewards democracy. Starratt (2003) states that "democratic leadership is primarily concerned to cultivate an environment that supports participation, sharing of ideas, and the virtues of honesty, openness, flexibility, and compassion" (p. 18). He argues that democratic school leadership should assist stakeholders in focusing their decision-making on the common good, developing the school as a testing ground for democratic life and leadership, and engaging in learning that contributes to building a democratic community.

Relationship of Democratic and Transformational Leadership

Whether democratic and transformational leadership are compatible with each other depends on the transformational model one chooses.

James MagGregor Burns' (1978) classic concept of transformational leadership certainly is democratic in nature:

> The premise of this leadership is that, whatever separate interests persons might hold, they are presently or potentially united in the pursuit of "higher" goals, the realization of which is tested by the achievement of significant change that represents the collective or pooled interests of leaders and followers.... Transformational leadership is more concerned with end-values, such as liberty, justice, equality. (pp. 425–426)

Denhardt and Campbell (2006), while agreeing that MacGregor Burns' view of transformational leadership is consistent with democratic leadership, discuss how conceptions of transformational leadership have become "bifurcated," with one camp continuing to support MacGregor Burns' perspective and another camp adopting a results-only perspective focused on the charismatic leader using the most efficient and effective means to convince others to accept change the leader believes is needed. Denhardt and Campbell argue in favor of MacGregor Burns model of transformational leadership:

> If we are committed to democratic governance, then it is no longer enough for leaders to come up with an idea and then work to convince others it is right. Instead, we need leaders who work with others to come up with the right ideas. (p. 569)

Green (1999) reminds us that transformational leadership can be negative or positive, citing Hitler and Stalin as negative examples. Green further argues that to be positive, transformation must be "deeply democratic, including all stakeholders in devising mutually satisfactory solutions to shared problems" (p. 216).

In their discussions of applying transformational leadership to schools, scholars like Shields (2018) and Hermanns and Berliner (2021) argue for the democratic version of transformational leadership, aiming to prepare students to be engaged citizens in a democratic society. In other words, the idea is to integrate transformational leadership with democratic leadership. Given the challenges associated with introducing democratic leadership discussed above, a combination of transformational and democratic leadership may be the best approach. For example, Makgato and Mudzanani (2019) found that leaders in schools with high student achievement demonstrated transformational *and* democratic leadership.

Structures and Processes for Democratic School Leadership

Before discussing structures and processes for democratic school leadership, some qualifications are in order. First, for these structures and processes to be effective, they must exist in a school culture where individuals value and respect each other and are willing to collaborate for the common good. Second, these structures and processes must be consistent with a school vision centered on democratic leadership, teaching, and learning to prepare citizens as full participants in a democratic society.

The *school council* is a popular structure for democratic leadership. In one version of democratic governance, each *stakeholder group* (teachers, students, students' families, the outside community served by the school) has its own governance body, each with democratically elected leaders, with members of each stakeholder group serving as representatives to the school council. Issues and recommendations from one or more stakeholder groups are brought before the school council for consideration. The school council can appoint committees, including members of different stakeholder groups, to study issues and develop proposals for council consideration.

Members of the school community can be invited to *open forums*, some regularly scheduled, some for the purpose of dealing with important concerns that have arisen (Furman & Starratt, 2005). Such forums may result in school improvement teams aimed at designing and implementing action plans, with those teams reporting to the school council and sharing progress at future forums. Regular *school assemblies* attended by educators and students can be used to share information, discuss issues, or make decisions. Teachers and students should be involved in planning and presenting at school assemblies. Regular small-scale student, teacher, family, or community *discussion groups* can be held at times convenient for the group involved. Breakfast, lunch, after-school, or evening discussion groups may best fit participants' schedules.

Some processes that can involve all stakeholders in democratic decision-making include vision building, curriculum development, instructional improvement, student learning, service to others, student assessment, action research, and program evaluation. Different stakeholders will have different roles in these various activities, but the democratic process should always apply.

Dialogue is an essential part of democratic decision-making. As Furman and Starratt (2005) note, democratic dialogue requires "the ability to listen, understand, empathize, negotiate, speak, debate, and resolve conflicts in a spirit of interdependence and working for the common good" (p. 118).

Teachers and Democratic Leadership

There are two prerequisites for teachers to become fully involved in democratic leadership. First, democratic leadership should relate to teachers' primary interests: teaching and student learning. Second, teachers must have material resources, time, and space for such leadership.

Once teachers see how their democratic leadership improves their work environment and student achievement, they will likely embrace that leadership as a critical aspect of their professional lives. Space does not allow a discussion of all the many types of teacher leadership, but a few examples are discussed below.

According to Castner et al., (2017), teachers' **democratic curriculum development** involves teachers asking critical questions about the curriculum and engaging in multiple types of reflective inquiry to answer those questions and revise the curriculum accordingly. This inquiry involves seeking the views of other stakeholders, including views that disagree with their own. It also includes reflecting on their own experiences in the classroom and in their lives outside the school. The goal is a curriculum that drives democratic classroom practice and results in higher-level learning for all students.

In **democratic professional development**, teachers decide on their learning needs, assist in planning professional learning activities, and engage in collaborative learning. In professional development described by Cate et al. (2006), teachers select workshops they wish to attend, share their learning with other teachers, and develop leadership skills that lead them to present at the local, regional, and state levels. Glickman et al. (2024) describe different forms of democratic peer assistance for professional learning, including peer observation, peer teaching, and peer coaching.

Democratic teacher evaluation involves teachers designing the evaluation criteria and process with the entire faculty providing input as well as reviewing and approving the evaluation system. Multiple observers gather teacher evaluation data and analyze those data in collaboration with the colleague being evaluated. The evaluated teacher works with colleagues to establish improvement goals and design a plan to meet those goals (Gordon, 2022). DiNota and Jebson (2011) and Sullivan (2012) describe examples of democratically developed teacher evaluation systems.

Democratic communities of practice are groups of individuals, often from different parts of an organization, who have a common interest or need and form a collaborative group that works together over time to address that interest or need (Wenger, 2009). Members of a community of practice in a K-12 school may come from different content areas or grade levels and be interested in areas like culturally responsive teaching, interdisciplinary curriculum, school culture, or restorative justice. Cate et al. (2006) found that the flow of information across different communities of practice supports schoolwide democracy.

Democratic teacher action research begins with a group of teachers selecting a focus area, usually related to improving teaching and learning. Teachers conduct initial data collection for two related purposes: to find out more about the area they have chosen to investigate and to generate ideas for improvement. Reviewing and discussing related literature can also provide knowledge about the focus area and ideas for moving forward.

Teachers next develop an action plan based on the data they have gathered and reflective dialogue. The action plan includes goals, improvement activities, and ways the teachers plan to assess action research outcomes. Teachers implement the action plan, assess results, and typically report findings to a larger audience. The action research cycle may be revised and repeated multiple times depending on the teachers' progress toward their stated goals or the development of new goals (Glickman et al., 2024).

Teachers' ***democratic classroom leadership*** involves transferring what they have learned about democratic leadership to the classroom by working with students to develop a democratic learning community (Jenlink & Jenlink, 2008). One example of the movement toward a democratic classroom proposed by Lloyd et al., (2016) involves the teacher shifting from deciding the topic, leading discussion, asking questions, and giving feedback to the teacher facilitating student discourse, listening to students, and encouraging students to listen to each other, and engaging students in dialogue in which all students' ideas are respected and valued.

Students and Democratic Leadership

Students need to be prepared for democratic leadership, preparation that will lead to a more positive school and classroom environment, improved student learning, and, ultimately, a more democratic society. Table 1.1 provides a partial list of areas where students should have input as part of the democratic process (Frost & Roberts, 2011; Quinn & Owen, 2016; Wallin, 2003). The types and degrees of input will be influenced by the developmental level of the students, with the general guideline that students should have as much input as their developmental level allows.

One way for students to have input is to complete schoolwide surveys asking for their opinions on school issues (Cate et al., 2006). A more interactive way is a student council, with self-nominated and democratically elected members and opportunities for representatives to present student input to the school council (Ralls, 2019). Democratic student leadership can

TABLE 1.1 Some Areas in Which Students Should Have Input	
Teacher-student relationships	Restorative justice
Student-student relationships	Campus physical environment
Curriculum	School safety
Teaching and learning activities	School culture
Student assessment	Co-curricular activities
Equity	Emerging school issues that affect students
Anti-bullying policies	School-community relations

involve students leading and/or presenting at morning assemblies (Cate et al., 2006), student forums, teacher-student forums (Frost & Roberts, 2011), and general meetings attended by educators, families, and other community members.

Students can suggest, debate, negotiate, and agree upon norms for a positive classroom learning environment. Small groups of students can engage in collaborative learning projects based on democratic principles. Students can participate in service learning to support a democratic school (e.g., improving the school culture, reducing violence) or community (e.g., assisting those in need, improving the neighborhood). Student service learning can be integrated with action research in which students identify a school or community problem, gather and interpret data on that problem, develop and implement an action plan, and assess and share the results of their efforts.

Families and Democratic Leadership

Pushor (2012) provides a rationale for democratic family involvement in their children's schooling:

> Parents' engagement in their children's education is a democratic right. Although raising student achievement is one of the legitimate aims of parent engagement, the democratic participation of parents in their children's schooling, through decision making and leadership processes that are representative and socially just, is a valued outcome in its own right. (p. 477)

The goals of family inclusion in democratic decision making include relationship building, removal of the power gap between the school and families, and the development of family leadership capacity. Additional goals are agreement on a shared school vision, family input into school policies and procedures that impact students, and collaborative work with educators to improve student learning (Epstein et al., 2002; Gordon, 2022; Pushor, 2012; Torre & Murphy, 2016).

In addition to traditional groups like parent-teacher associations, students' family members should be elected representatives on the school council and serve on advisory groups and committees appointed by the school council (Epstein et al., 2002). Family networks can include all who wish to join, with network leaders liaising between the school and network members (Epstein et al., 2002; Gordon, 2022). Family centers can be located on campus and coordinated by family members (Auerbach, 2010). These centers can provide office space for center leadership and workspace for family members assisting teachers and students. Family centers can host discussion groups, family education programs, and action teams, and provide resources for students and their families.

Students' family members can engage in various activities preparing them to be democratic leaders. Auerbach (2010) describes types of preparation such as academies designed to help families understand their rights and responsibilities, leadership training, workshops based on family-perceived needs, and joining teachers in professional development programs. Examples of leadership activities for family members include presentations to the school community; collaborative curriculum development with teachers and other stakeholders (Pushor, 2012); in-school and at-home work with teachers to assist student learning (Gordon, 2022); and expert-assisted, family-led action research to improve the school or community (Ippolito, 2010).

Scholars have identified characteristics of democratic school-family partnerships (Epstein et al., 2002; Gordon, 2022; Pushor, 2012; Torre & Murphy, 2016). In such partnership, educators and families respect one another, treat each other as equals, and focus on the improvement of student learning. Families have input regarding all major decisions that affect their children, and educators and families accept collective responsibility for implementing those decisions. Educators and families share information about students and educational efforts at school and at home, complementing each other. Family members assisting at school engage in meaningful activities to assist student learning. Democratic school-family partnership grows over time, with more families becoming involved in different types of democratic leadership.

The Community and Democratic Leadership

All community members served by the school should be invited to participate in democratic leadership. There are many ways a school can invite and benefit from such leadership. A school website can enable two-way communication in which community citizens are kept up to date on school issues and initiatives and provided opportunities for input. Participants in school-community forums can express alternative views and engage in dialogue on issues affecting the school and the community. Educators can go into the community to visit community leaders and other citizens to discuss school and community concerns and the relationship between those concerns. Community members committed to improving student learning can be invited into the school to consult with and assist teachers in democratic pedagogy.

Two formal types of democratic leadership involving community members are the school-community council and school-community partnerships. The *school-community council* includes democratically elected community members, with representatives from that council joining representatives of other stakeholder groups on the school council. *School-community partnerships* "improve the quality of education by raising the quality of life for everyone in the community" (FitzGerald & Quiñones, 2019, p. 525). Democratic partnerships can include a single or multiple community partners depending on the purpose of the partnership, with all partners considered equal, and all contributing to and benefitting from the partnership.

Examples of typical community partners include health organizations, businesses, youth organizations, public libraries, art centers, social service agencies, museums, and universities (Bryon & Henry, 2012; FitzGerald & Quiñones, 2019).

Democratic school-community partnerships have myriad purposes. A few examples include:

- physical and emotional health services for students
- school-based distribution centers with food and clothing for students and their families
- adults from the community tutoring students or facilitating small-group learning
- provision of learning resources and materials to students
- after-school educational and recreational programs for students
- after-school adult education in school facilities
- apprenticeships for students in community organizations
- educators, students, and community members joining in service projects to support community members in need
- educators, students, and community members engaged in action research to promote school and community equity.

All the above purposes can be met through a partnership of school and community members democratically assessing school *and* community needs and then planning, implementing, and monitoring partnership efforts to meet those needs.

Democratic school-community partnerships should be reciprocal, but what exactly does reciprocity mean? Dostilio et al. (2012) propose three orientations to reciprocity: exchange, influence, and generativity. *Exchange* means that the partners each provide and gain something from the partnership. *Influence* means that, as the partnership continues, both its process and outcomes change due to each partner's influence. *Generativity* means that together the partners become or create something new that would not exist without the partnership.

Benefits of Democratic School Leadership and Democratic Schools

Democratic leadership (by multiple stakeholders) is essential for democratic schools, but is a democratic school worth all the effort necessary to make it a reality? Regarding the *school environment*, democracy results in a more inclusive, supportive, and collaborative school environment, leading to a sense of belonging for all members of the school community (Uy et al., 2024). Democratic schools increase trust, empowerment, and commitment among all stakeholders (San Antonio, 2008). Equity increases in a democratic school environment (Uy et al., 2024; Williams et al., 2009), as does service to others with a view toward the common good (Williams et al., 2009). Democracy promotes a community of critical thinkers and reflective learners (Fetterman, 2017). Members of a democratic school community believe they have more influence in decision-making (Wahlstrom et al., 2010), and changes implemented in a democratic school are more likely to be maintained (Brough, 2012).

A democratic school has multiple benefits for ***teachers***. Democracy cultivates teacher trust, collaboration, professional growth, and creativity, increasing teacher morale, job satisfaction, commitment, and retention (Uy et al., 2024). In a democratic school, teachers become more learner-centered and develop leadership skills (Williams et al., 2009). The democratic process helps teachers build positive relationships with students, colleagues, their students' families, and other members of the community served by the school (Wahlstrom et al., 2010). And, in relation to all the above, a democratic environment helps teachers to improve their teaching (Waldron & McLeskey, 2010).

Democratic schools foster a host of positive dispositions, behaviors, and outcomes for ***students***. These schools increase students' sense of being valued (Hope, 2012), belonging to the school community, self-efficacy, and motivation (Uy et al., 2024). A democratic school community enhances students' self-concept as well as their trust of one another (Wallin, 2003). A democratic learning environment assists students in accepting ownership of their learning, actively engaging in learning (Brough, 2012), and considering their learning a positive experience (Wallin, 2003). More specifically, a democratic school helps students to identify learning goals, plan learning experiences, and self-assess their progress (Wallin, 2003). Democratic schools promote both student leadership and collaboration (Williams et al., 2009), and students in such schools are more likely to show tolerance toward, have a constructive influence on (Wallin, 2003), and develop positive relationships (Hope, 2012) with other students. As a result of being educated in a democratic school, students are more likely to improve their academic achievement (Uy et al., 2024; Wahlstrom et al., 2010; Waldron & McLeskey, 2010) as well as develop their social skills, problem-solving ability, critical thinking (Quinn & Owen, 2016), and creativity (Wallin, 2003). Moreover, students who learn through a democratic process are more likely to apply and retain their learning (Bough, 2012).

Democratic schools have benefits for ***families*** and school-family relationships. A democratic approach means families are better informed about teachers' goals and student needs (LaRocque et al., 2011) and have increased efficacy and capacity to assist student learning (Torre & Murphy, 2016). Families are more likely to be engaged with, satisfied with, and supportive of democratic schools (LaRocque et al., 2011; Warren, 2005). Democratic schools are particularly important for families from historically marginalized groups, as part of the democratic process involves working with families for equity, social justice, and empowerment inside and outside the school (Ippolito, 2010).

Democratic schools also benefit the *community* and school-community partnership. A democratic approach improves school-community relations (Wallin, 2003), and communities are more engaged with and provide greater support for democratic schools (Uy et al., 2024). A democratic school can place itself at the center of efforts to empower the community and provide equity for all its members (Bryon & Henry, 2012; Warren, 2005).

One area that lacks sufficient research and needs to be studied more concerns the effects of democratic leadership and democratic schools on society. After all, the long-range purpose of democratic schools is to prepare students to be active citizens in a democratic society. Do students carry democratic beliefs and behaviors they develop in a democratic school into their adult lives? Do they actively support democracy at the interpersonal, community, and national levels? Research on this topic could involve gathering data on the level of democracy citizens were exposed to in school and comparing it to their adult beliefs and actions concerning democracy.

PRACTICAL IMPLICATIONS FOR PROMOTING DEMOCRATIC SCHOOL LEADERSHIP

The following implications are provided for practitioners committed to democratic leadership and democratic schools:

- Begin by engaging stakeholders in dialogue on the meaning of deep democracy and its value to all school community members.
- Offer professional development on democratic leadership to faculty and staff, and adult learning on democratic leadership to students' families and other members of the community served by the school.
- Include democracy and democratic leadership in the school vision.
- Integrate democracy and democratic leadership across the school curriculum.
- Engage students in as much democracy and democratic leadership as their developmental level allows.
- Aim to increase democracy and democratic leadership over time by including more stakeholders in more types of democratic decision-making.

CONCLUSION

Several general observations about democratic leadership and democratic schools can be made. First, most K-12 schools are not centers of deep democracy. Second, given the history and existing organizational structure of schools, it is difficult to transform a conventional school into a democratic school. Third, such a transition, although difficult, can take place. Most of the democratic schools described in the literature were typical schools with typical staffs serving typical communities prior to becoming democratic. In most cases, the move toward democracy has been initiated by a principal engaged in both transformational *and* democratic leadership. Finally, the positive effects of democratic school leadership tend to cause such leadership to be accepted by stakeholders and gradually distributed across the school community, with support for democracy continuing over time.

CASE STUDY

Maria Garza is preparing for her first year as principal at Lakeside Middle School, a grade 6-8 school in a large city suburb. The school serves a local community that is racially, ethnically, and economically diverse, with student demographics that reflect the community. Approximately one-fourth of the teachers at Lakeside are near the end of their careers, one-half of the faculty is mid-career, and one-fourth of the teachers are in their first three years of teaching. The former principal at Lakeside had led the school for many years, and his leadership style—toward teachers, students, and families—was decidedly "top-down." The retiring principal's communication with students' families and other community members was limited to short welcoming addresses at "back-to-school-nights" and occasional brief talks at community events. Teacher-family communication at Lakeside has consisted primarily of semi-annual family-teacher conferences on student progress and meetings requested by teachers to address problems with an individual student's behavior or academic performance. There is a parent-teacher association, but in recent years, its infrequent meetings have led to low attendance. The area served by the school is largely residential, but it includes a shopping center, hospital, early childhood center, computer consulting firm, and residence for the elderly. There is a major university located in the city, ten miles north of the middle school.

Maria is strongly committed to democratic school leadership and involving others in such leadership, which are commitments she made clear during the interview process for her new position. During the interview process, she learned that district leadership was interested in introducing service learning at all school levels but is in the early stages of what will be a major change for district schools. Maria believes that democratic leadership and service learning would be a natural combination. However, she also understands that the conventional leadership Lakeside has experienced over many years will make such innovations challenging.

REFLECTIONS ON THE CASE

- How could Maria introduce ideas for integrating democratic leadership and service learning for consideration by stakeholders in Lakeside Middle School?
- What types of professional development on democratic leadership could Maria offer to teachers and staff? What types of adult education on democratic leadership could Maria offer to students' families and other community members?
- How could stakeholders in Lakeside integrate democratic leadership and service learning in mutually supportive ways?

REFERENCES

Alderson, P. (2004). Democracy in schools: Myths, mirages and making it happen. In B. Linsley & E. Rayment (Eds.), *Beyond the classroom: Exploring active citizenship in 11–16 education* (pp. 31–38). New Politics Network.

Auerbach, S. (2010). Beyond coffee with the principal: Toward leadership for authentic school-family partnerships. *Journal of School Leadership, 20*, 728–757. https://doi.org/10.1177/105268461002000603

Brough, C. J. (2012). Implementing the democratic principles and practices of student-centered curriculum integration in primary schools. *Curriculum Journal, 23*(3), 345–369. https://doi.org/10.1080/09585176.2012.703498

Bryon, J., & Henry, L. (2012). A model for building school-family-community partnerships: Principles and process. *Journal of Counseling & Development, 90*(4), 408–420. https://doi.org/10.1002/j.1556-6676.2012.00052.x

Burns, J. M. (1978). *Leadership*. Harper & Row.

Castner, D. J., Schneider, J. L., & Henderson, J. G. (2017). An ethnic of democratic, curriculum-based teacher leadership. *Leadership and Policy in Schools, 16*(2), 328–356. https://doi.org/10.1080/15700763.2017.1298814

Cate, J. M., Vaughn, C. A., & O'Hair, M. J. (2006). A 17-year case study of an elementary school's journey: From traditional school to learning community to democratic school community. *Journal of School Leadership, 16*(1), 86–111. https://doi.org/10.1177/105268460601600104

Denhardt, J. V., & Campbell, K. B. (2006). The role of democratic values in transformational leadership. *Administration & Society, 38*(5), 556–572. https://doi.org/10.1177/00953997062897

Dewey, J. (1916). *Democracy and education*. Free Press.

DiNota, C., & Jebson, H. (2011). Trust, accountability, autonomy. *Independent School, 70*(4). https://www.nais.org/magazine/independent-school/summer-2011/trust,-accountability,-autonomy/

Dostilio, L. D., Brackmann, S. M., Edwards, K. E., Harrision, B., Kliewer, B. W., & Clayton, P. H. (2012). Reciprocity: Saying what we mean and meaning what we say. *Michigan Journal of Community Service Learning, 19*(1), 17–32. http://hdl.handle.net/2027/spo.3239521.0019.102

Epstein, J. L., Sanders, M. G., Simon, B. S., Salinas, K. C., Jansorn, N. R., Van Voorhis, F. L..(2002). *School, family, and community partnerships: Your handbook for action* (2nd ed.). Corwin Press.

Fetterman, D. (2017). Transformative empowerment evaluation and Freirean pedagogy: Alignment with an emancipatory tradition. In M. Q. Patton (Ed.), *Pedagogy of evaluation: New directions for evaluation,* (*2017*(155), pp. 111–126). https://doi.org/10.1002/ev.20257

FitzGerald, A. M., & Quiñones, S. (2019). Working in and with community: Leading for partnerships in a community school. *Leadership and Policy in Schools, 18*(4), 511–532. https://doi.org/10.1080/15700763.2018.1453938

Frost, D., & Roberts, A. (2011). Student leadership, participation and democracy. *Leading and Managing, 17*(2), 66–84.

Furman, G. C., & Starratt, R. J. (2005). Leadership for democratic community in schools. In J. Murphy (Ed.), *The educational leadership challenge: Redefining leadership for the 21st century: 101st yearbook of the National Society for the Study of Education* (pp. 105–133). University of Chicago Press.

Gerstl-Pepin, C., & Aiken, J. A. (2009). Democratic school leaders: Defining ethical leadership in a standardized context. *Journal of School Leadership, 19*(4), 406–444. https://doi.org/10.1177/105268460901900402

Glickman, C. D., Gordon, S. P., Ross-Gordon, J. M., & Solis, R. D. (2024). *Supervision and instructional leadership: A developmental approach* (11th ed.). Pearson.

Glickman, C. D., & Mette, I. M. (2020). *The essential renewal of America's schools: A leadership guide for democratizing schools from the inside out.* Teachers College Press.

Gordon, S. P. (2022). *Developing successful schools: A holistic approach.* Palgrave Macmillan.

Gordon, S. P., & Boone, M. (2014). *Alternative approaches to educational leadership preparation: A call for integration.* National Council of Professors of Educational Administration.

Green, J. M. (1999). *Deep democracy: Community, diversity, and transformation.* Rowman & Littlefield.

Harris, A., & Chapman, C. (2002). Democratic leadership for school improvement in challenging contexts. *International Electronic Journal for Leadership in Learning, 6*(9). http://eprints.gla.ac.uk/75099/

Hermanns, C., & Berliner, D. C. (2021). Leadership for democratic education in troubled times. *eJournal of Education Policy, 21*(1). https://in.nau.edu/wpcontent/uploads/sites/135/2021/12/Hermanns_et_al.pdf

Hope, M. A. (2012). The importance of belonging: Learning from the student experience of democratic education. *Journal of School Leadership, 22*(4), 733–750. https://doi.org/10.1177/105268461202200403

Ippolito, J. (2010). Minority parents as researchers: Beyond a dichotomy in parent involvement in schooling. *Canadian Journal of Educational Administration and Policy, 2010*(114), 47–68.

James, B. J. (2010). Reclaiming deep democracy. *Reclaiming Children and Youth: Journal of Emotional and Behavioral Problems, 19*(3), 16–19.

Jenlink, P. M., & Jenlink, E. (2008). Creating democratic learning communities: Transformative work as spatial practice. *Theory into Practice, 47*(4), 311–317. https://doi.org/10.1080/00405840802329300

Kadivar, M. A., Usmani, A., & Bradlow, B. H. (2020). The long march: Deep democracy in cross-national perspective. *Social Forces, 98*(3), 1311–1338. https://doi.org/10.1093/sf/soz050

Klinker, J. (2006). Qualities of democracy: Links to democratic leadership. *Journal of Thought, 41*(2), 51–63. https://www.jstor.org/stable/42589867

LaRocque, M., Kleiman, I., & Darling, S. M. (2011). Parental involvement: The missing link in school achievement. *Preventing School Failure, 55*(3), 115–122. https://doi.org/10.1080/10459880903472876

Larsen, E. (2024). Mission and mandates: School leaders' and teachers' professional discretion in enacting education for democracy. *International Journal of Leadership in Education, 27*(3), 661–685. https://doi.org/10.1080/13603124.2021.1893390

Lloyd, M. H., Kolodziej, N. J., & Brashears, K. M. (2016). Classroom discourse: An essential component in building a classroom community. *School Community Journal, 26*(2), 291-304. http://www.schoolcommunitynetwork.org/SCJ.aspx

Makgato, M., & Mudzanani, N. N. (2019). Exploring school principals' leadership styles and learners' educational performance: A perspective from high- and low-performing schools. *Africa Education Review, 16*(2), 90–108. https://doi.org/10.1080/18146627.2017.1411201

Pushor, D. (2012). Tracing my research on parent engagement: Working to interrupt the story of school as protectorate. *Action in Teacher Education, 34*(5–6), 464–479. https://doi.org/10.1080/01626620.2012.729474

Quinn, S., & Owen, S. (2016). Digging deeper: Understanding the power of 'student voice'. *Australian Journal of Education, 60*(1), 60-72. https://doi.org/10.1177/0004944115626402

Ralls, D. (2019). 'Becoming co-operative'—Challenges and insights: Repositioning school engagement as a collective endeavour. *International Journal of Inclusive Education, 23*(11), 1134–1138. https://doi.org/10.1080/13603116.2019.1629159

San Antonio, D. M. (2008). Creating better schools through democratic school leadership. *International Journal of Leadership in Education, 11*(1), 43–62. https://doi.org/10.1080/13603120601174311

Shields, C. M. (2018). *Transformative leadership in education* (2nd ed.). Routledge.

Starratt, R. J. (2003). Democratic leadership theory in late modernity: An oxymoron or ironic possibility? In P. T. Begley & O. Johansson (Eds.), *The ethical dimensions of school leadership* (pp. 13–31). Kluwer Academic Publishers.

Sullivan, J. P. (2012). A collaborative effort: Peer review and the history of teacher evaluations in Montgomery County, Maryland. *Harvard Educational Review, 82*(1), 142–152.

Torre, D., & Murphy, J. (2016). Communities of parent engagement: New foundations for school leaders' work. *International Journal of Leadership in Education, 19*(2), 203–223. https://doi.org/10.1080/13603124.2014.958200

Uy, F. T., Andrin, G. R., Vestal, P. E., Malbas, M. H., Barcelo, M. N. A., & Kilag, O. K. T. (2024). Empowering education: The impact of democratic school leadership on educational outcome. *International Multidisciplinary Journal of Research for Innovation, Sustainability, and Excellence (IMJRISE), 1*(3), 178–184.

Wahlstrom, K. L., Louis, K. S., Leithwood, K., & Anderson, S. E. (2010). *Investigating the links to improved student learning: Executive summary of research findings.* Wallace Foundation.

Waldron, N. L., & McLeskey, J. (2010). Establishing a collaborative school culture through comprehensive school reform. *Journal of Educational and Psychological Consultation, 20*(1), 58–74. https://doi.org/10.1080/10474410903535364

Wallin, D. (2003). Student leadership and democratic schools: A case study. *NASSP Bulletin, 87*(636), 55–78. https://doi.org/10.1177/019263650308763606

Warren, M. R. (2005). Communities and schools: A new view of urban education reform. *Harvard Educational Review, 75*(2), 133–173. https://doi.org/10.17763/haer.75.2.m718151032167438

Wenger, E. (2009). A social theory of learning. In K. Illeris (Ed.), *Contemporary theories of learning: Learning theorists . . . in their own words* (pp. 200–208). Routledge.

Williams, L., Cate, J., & O'Hair, M. J. (2009). The boundary-spanning role of democratic learning communities: Implementing the IDEALS. *Educational Management Administration & Leadership, 37*(4), 452–472. https://doi.org/10.1177/1741143209334580

Woods, P. A. (2021). Democratic leadership. In R. Papa (Ed.), *Oxford encyclopedia of educational administration.* Oxford University Press.

Young, I. M. (2000). *Inclusion and democracy.* Oxford University Press.

CHAPTER 2

CREATING CHANGE THROUGH DEVELOPING A GROWTH MINDSET IN A LARGE HIGH SCHOOL

Lee Westberry
Citadel Military College, USA

ABSTRACT

In Chapter 2, Professor Westberry focuses on creating a singular school culture of continuous growth at the high school level. She posits that change is never easy, and cultural change can be the hardest to create. High school content area teachers often cluster together and isolate themselves from others in the building. Thus, the challenge of creating cohesion and a growth mindset among all faculty requires a transformational leader. The chapter presents an actual attempt to alter the culture of a large high school, from maintaining the status quo to developing a growth mindset among all faculty. This change was aimed to increase improvements in student achievement and increase collective self-efficacy among staff members. Challenges faced, mistakes, and lessons learned are shared in this chapter. Specific examples are given in the areas of creating a shared vision, building a culture of collaboration, and empowering teachers to lead—all tenets of transformational leadership.

Keywords: Cultural change; visionary leadership; transformational leaders; high schools in crises; colleges; further education

> *Prefocus Guiding Questions*
>
> - *What type of leadership skills/styles are best suited to develop a growth mindset?*
> - *How do you develop collective self-efficacy in a large school?*
> - *How can teacher leaders be actualized to create a learning culture?*

INTRODUCTION

Today's school leaders face so many challenges that leaders just 10 years ago never imagined. Once upon a time, school leaders were deemed successful if they effectively managed the school buildings and the people within. This is no longer the case. Administrators today must effectively manage and lead; this leadership is the basis of many research studies and graduate-level courses. What constitutes an effective school leader? The answer would depend on the school culture one wants to create.

One of the newer challenges for school leaders is to lead teachers in their growth and development to impact student achievement results positively. Now, one can be an instructional leader and not garner the desired impact. How is this possible? Well, one can proclaim instructional leadership by merely dictating expected instructional practices and monitoring their progress. For example, lesson plans are to be submitted each Friday for review. This is an instructional practice that, honestly, is underutilized in schools. However, this practice alone will not garner teacher growth. Instructional supervision intends to grow and develop teachers' instructional practices (Glickman et al., 2017; Zepeda, 2018), not just develop compliance in teachers based on instructional demands. So, for lesson plan review to have any impact, feedback must be given in a constructive, consistent manner that helps mold practices in teachers.

Developing a learning culture among teachers is the most complex challenge. To truly develop a growth mindset or a desire to learn (Dweck, 2007; Yeager & Dweck, 2020) among teachers that results in collective self-efficacy or the belief in the collective ability of the school (Bandura, 1977; Donohoo et al., 2018; Hattie & Zierer, 2018) is the ultimate goal of instructional supervision. Is it achievable? Yes, it is. Is it easy? No, it is not. This paradigm change must be planned using effective leadership skills and teacher leadership.

LEADERSHIP

Leadership Styles

Many aspiring leaders ask what leadership skills are essential to running an effective and efficient school. Researchers have defined many types of

TABLE 2.1 Tenets of Leadership Styles		
Leadership Style	Tenets	Source
Transactional	Utilizes rewards and punishments for motivation; very top-down with a clear structure.	Burns (1978) Bass and Avolio (1993)
Laissez Faire	Very hands-off; people make their own decisions with little interference.	Robbins et al. (2007) Bartol and Martin (1994)
Participative	Employee feedback is sought to make decisions, democratic in nature and shared power.	Likert (1961)
Servant	Shared power puts the needs of employees first rather than of the organization.	Greenleaf (2003)
Distributed	Shared decision-making authority: collaborative but extended across the organization.	Gibb (1954)
Transformational	Inspires positive change in others to benefit the individuals as well as the organization through shared vision; fosters ownership among the members that activates a call to action.	Burns (1978) Avolio et al. (1991) Leithwood and Jantzi (2006)

leadership styles: transactional, participative, laissez-faire, servant, distributed, and transformational, to name a few. See Table 2.1 above for the main tenets of some and a useful source for further study.

These theories are critical, but in isolation, the application of these leadership styles does not net results simply because people are complex beings. Ideally, a leader would possess all of these leadership styles and know when to use them. Yes, teachers are asked to differentiate instruction daily, and administrators should differentiate leadership styles based on the needs of the people they are trying to lead. Consider the following example.

At a large high school with 150 teachers, it is not very responsible to think that all 150 people have the exact needs. For example, *Mrs. Ann*, an English teacher who has been teaching for over 20 years, does not have the exact needs of *Ms. Jennifer*, a first-year teacher. Mrs. Jennifer may need more direct support in understanding expectations and how to meet them successfully, while Mrs. Ann may need more voice in school-based decisions. Then consider *Mrs. Pam*, who is very negative during all teacher meetings. It is clear to all around her that she does not like the children she teaches or teaching in general. Mrs. Pam needs clear expectations and close progress monitoring for the sake of the students she teaches.

Suffice it to say that when administrators are asked about their leadership styles, one answer does not fit all. The correct answer would be to use a differentiated leadership approach. Nevertheless, school leaders feel compelled to say they are transformational and collaborative because they feel that is what is expected of them. It is essential to know yourself and the people you are trying to lead so that you can meet their needs. If not, you are not leading anyone. A leadership style studied in isolation is fruitless. The perfect analogy to this type of study is that you are fluent in reading data but do not know how to use it to improve outcomes.

Fuller's Stages of Concern

Another consideration of teachers is their stage of concern or what is driving them. For those considerations, Frances Fuller's (1969) Stages of Concern must play a part. See Table 2.2 below for the Stages of Concern and their impact on teachers.

All teachers will fall into one or more of these categories at different times. Yes, one teacher can rotate between stages in the same year. For this reason, school leaders must understand what is driving their teachers and why. Only then can the appropriate leadership style be utilized. Consider the same individuals in the large high school above.

> Mrs. Ann, a 20-year veteran, has just been told that she has to incorporate an online learning management system and is not computer savvy. As such, Mrs. Ann is very anxious and intimidated by the demand. Before the new district mandate, Mrs. Ann was focused on student learning and differentiating her instruction to meet the needs of her students best. Now, however, she is feeling like a fish out of water. Mrs. Ann moved from the teacher Impact Stage of Concern to the Self-Stage of Concern (Fuller, 1969) in that she is focused on her adequacy with the use of technology.

Where you were able to use more of the participative leadership style with Mrs. Ann in the past, you now may need to employ more transformational leadership skills to motivate teachers to own the needed change coupled with some distributive leadership skills so that Mrs. Ann gets the support she needs from those more proficient in the use of technology.

TABLE 2.2 Fuller's Stages of Concern (1969)	
Stage	Impact
Self	Teachers are more concerned with survival and self-adequacy.
Task	Teachers are more concerned about fulfilling teacher duties and student performance.
Impact	Teachers self-reflect on the effectiveness of their teaching and turn the focus to student learning.

Ms. Jennifer, a first-year teacher who started the year in the Self-Concern Stage (Fuller, 1969) and was trying to survive her first year of teaching, was excited about the online learning management system. She loves technology and wants to share her knowledge with her peers. She feels that helping her colleagues with the transition will make her a valued part of the team.

While at the beginning of the year, Ms. Jennifer required a more directive approach to supervision, with the addition of technology, one may use a more collaborative approach with transformational leadership and distributed leadership skills. The change will motivate and utilize Ms. Jennifer's skills to the benefit of all.

Mrs. Pam, the tenured negative Nelly, thinks that the new technology mandate will soon pass and there is no need to learn something new. She does not understand why teachers must use technology to engage students further. She feels that students should do what they are instructed to do. Besides, technology will not motivate students to do their work. Nothing will change if their parents do not hold them accountable at home. With Mrs. Pam, the transactional form of leadership will be most effective until she starts to see results. However, Mrs. Pam may never change her category of teacher.

Categories of Teachers

In this researcher's estimation, based on 20+ years of administrative experience, there are three simple categories of teachers: speedboats, sailboats, and U-boats. See Figure 2.1 for a depiction of the categories. Administrators need to understand these categories to better understand their staff and know what leadership skills to employ for maximum effectiveness.

Speedboats only need gas and are pointed in the right direction. They will take off and make the most of any innovation for the benefit of their students. School leaders must check in with them and use a more participative and distributed leadership style. However, it is important to note that not all teachers can move at the same pace as these speedboats, so school leaders must be careful how they are utilized in leadership positions so these teacher leaders are not shunned by their peers. Typically, about 10% of a faculty is comprised of speedboats, with more if an administrator is lucky! Speedboats, working in collaboration with others, are excellent support for sailboats.

The vast majority of teachers are sailboats, typically around 80%. These teachers want what is best for their students, but they may be uncertain, vacillating between Fuller's Stages of Concern (1969). They want to be effective and confident in their craft and take things slower. Sometimes, it takes them longer to get on board with a new program, but they eventually will get there with the right support.

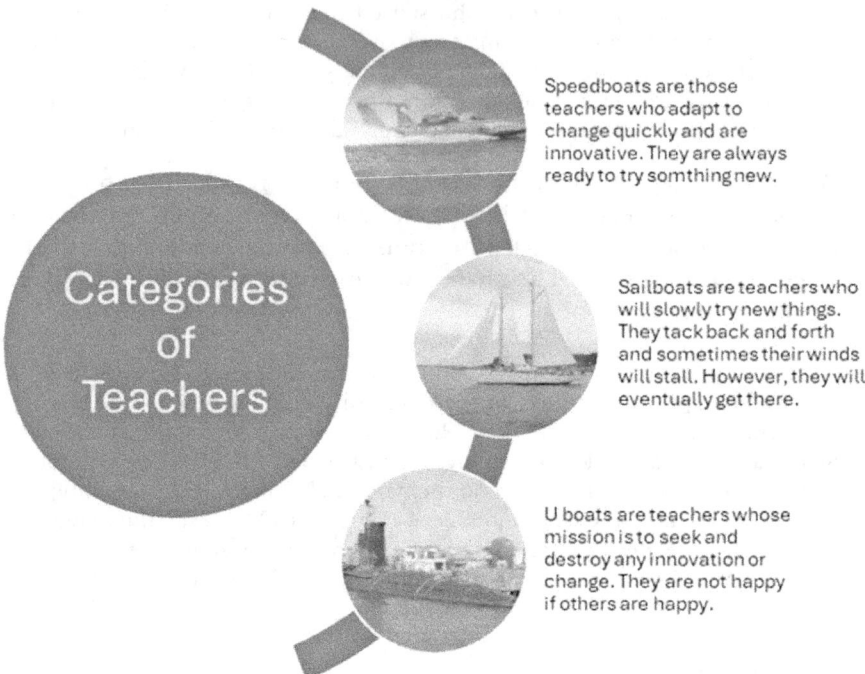

Figure 2.1 Categories of teachers.

The last category of teachers is the U-boat. These teachers oppose any change as they are traditional and are set in their ways. They are generally unhappy and do not like the changes seen in students and society's culture today. Their mission is to derail any new program as it is seen as a threat. These teachers, however, need an audience to thrive. Without an audience, they become isolated, and U-boats cannot survive in isolation. Therefore, they are constantly seeking other teachers to get them to agree. Sailboats whose winds have stalled and those in the Self-Stage of Concern (Fuller, 1969) are the usual targets as they are considered low-hanging fruit.

Understanding these categories of teachers is essential. School leaders should spend the majority of their time with the sailboats, wrapping them with support while checking in with the speedboats. In this scenario, U-boats either conform or leave. Either is acceptable. However, if you can determine the motivation for the u boat, it is important to address the concern. Consider the following scenario.

> Mrs. Karen, a veteran English teacher who taught freshman English, seemed angry. She was a sound teacher with good, basic pedagogy who frequently garnered good test results from her students. However, these students often

complained about Mrs. Karen's strictness and that her class was no fun. Schedule change requests often were submitted to guidance, with students looking for any other 9th-grade English teacher. Mrs. Karen often complained in her teacher teams and never wanted to try anything new to reach her students and engage them further.

The large high school's new administration observed Mrs. Karen for a while and saw that she was firm in her content and teaching skills, but it appeared the team did not value Mrs. Karen's input because they were tired of her negativity. The principal decided to talk to Mrs. Karen and find out what she believed was the problem. During that conversation, Mrs. Karen revealed she was upset with the prior school administration and the current administration by default. Mrs. Karen felt she had the most teaching experience in her department and had earned the right to teach senior English and Advanced Placement English; however, she was stuck teaching freshmen. After hearing her complaint, the administration understood why Mrs. Karen was a U-boat. The principal gave Mrs. Karen a schedule with upperclassmen for one semester and then monitored the state testing results. Mrs. Karen was ecstatic and seemed happier that someone had listened to her. At the end of the semester, the principal conducted a data analysis and called Mrs. Karen in for a conference. The data showed that Mrs. Karen was the staff's most effective with freshman English. As a result, the administration expressed their need for Mrs. Karen to teach freshman English. The principal expresses that teaching 9th grade was not an oversight but a declaration of teacher effectiveness. Mrs. Karen stood even taller as she finally understood that she was valued. She contributed more positively and volunteered to lead the professional development (PD) of teaching strategies. Mrs. Karen moved to the sailboat category because someone bothered to discover her motivation for being a U-boat. Therefore, Mrs. Karen's leadership style changed from transactional to transformative and participatory.

In essence, school leaders must possess all the tools in their toolbelts to lead effectively. They must understand the different leadership skills and how to differentiate them to meet the needs of those they are trying to lead. They must also understand the stages of concern (Fuller, 1969) of teachers, the categories of teachers, and how that will impact the leadership skills needed to be effective. One size does not fit all, and the size is bound to change multiple times in one school year.

Self-Efficacy

After knowing about your teachers and the leadership skills needed, one must then turn to teacher effectiveness. The link between teachers' effectiveness and teaching practices can be rooted in self-efficacy. Lee and Bobko (1994) studied Bandura's (1986) concept of self-efficacy and stated,

> Those who have a strong sense of self-efficacy in a particular situation will devote their attention and effort to the demands of the situation, and when faced with obstacles and difficult situations, these individuals will try harder and persist longer. (p. 364)

At its core, self-efficacy is a social cognitive theory that states the degree to which an individual believes his/her abilities will dictate his/her effectiveness accordingly (Bandura, 1997). Three major assumptions exist with this social cognitive theory:

1. People can learn by observing others, even if prior experience is lacking.
2. Reinforcement is the key to learning, both externally and internally. Intrinsic motivation achieves mental preparedness to learn.
3. Self-regulation is necessary to sustain change; changed behaviors do not necessarily result from new learning (Bandura, 1991).

The leadership skills needed are imperative when thinking about teachers' self-efficacy and how to develop it. Three basic assumptions to consider on the path to building the self-efficacy of teachers include the following:

1. A sound system of curriculum and instruction is mandatory. This is "...the basis of a successful school and must be developed and refined along with a system of instructional supervision" (Westberry, 2020, p. 19).
2. Teachers may be confident in their content knowledge but may not be confident in their pedagogy (Lewis, 2009; Tygret, 2018).
3. A robust system of teacher support is needed to include relevant and timely PD in which teachers can see the positive effects (Lessing & De Witt, 2007) and must include all four cycles of PD (Westberry, 2020).

The four cycles of PD (Westberry, 2020) include the following:

1. All teacher PD—PD that all teachers need to move the school's strategic plan forward. For example, all teachers may work on intervention strategies to support struggling learners.
2. New teacher PD—This PD is intended for teachers new to the profession and new to the building. Tenured teachers received this training in prior years, and to maintain fidelity of expectation and implementation, the PD must be repeated for all newcomers

each year. This PD is essential to the school's academic program. For example, writing across the curriculum may need repeating each year for new teachers. Without this cycle, implementation fidelity erodes over time, and programs fail. Often, this is what creates the hamster wheel of programs in schools.
3. Focus teacher PD—This PD is intended for small groups of teachers. For example, new math standards may require PD for math teachers only or classroom management PD for teachers struggling in this area.
4. Professional Learning Communities (PLCs)—If done correctly, PLCs provide great professional learning. This avenue is perfect for data analysis, lesson planning, assessment building, and examination of student work.

All four cycles of PD should be running concurrently throughout a school year to provide the support needed for teachers to feel confident in their practice and meet expectations. In order to effectively impact the level of confidence needed by teachers today, administrators must utilize all leadership skills to meet the needs of all of the teachers who may be in different stages and categories. Consider the following:

> At the same large high school with a staff of nearly 150 teachers, the principal wanted to create a system of curriculum and instruction that supported teachers in their growth. To do so, the principal needed to conduct an instructional needs assessment to determine the needs of the teachers based on careful examination through observation document review to include assessments, lesson plans, PLC feedback forms, and test data. After sharing the information needed with the leadership team, the principal utilized distributive leadership to share the work. By doing this, teachers could see the needs themselves rather than being told their needs. Patterns of behavior were highlighted to help develop the PD plan for the school. Participatory leadership skills were utilized to hear teacher concerns and ideas about the PD to come. All ideas were welcome. Once a plan was agreed upon, the principal utilized transformational leadership skills to share the vision and set the goals for growth with the faculty. Teachers understood the need for PD and valued the learning. They were anxious to incorporate the learning in the classroom to see the impact on student outcomes.

Though this scenario may seem idyllic, it is a real-life scenario in a high school of nearly 2,000 students. Once teachers started feeling confident and seeing the results, the faculty took the next step. Remember, self-efficacy is established by the following:

1. Learning through observing others. PD provides these opportunities for teachers to learn from each other.

2. Providing reinforcement, both externally and internally. When implemented, PD provides for mental preparedness and opportunities for praise.
3. PD in PLCs provides for change to be sustained through collaboration and discourse as teachers support one another (Bandura, 1991).

Once self-efficacy is built within teachers, the next step is to move to collective self-efficacy.

Collective Self-Efficacy

Building on Albert Bandura's work from the 1990s, where he found that the group's shared belief in the organization's abilities impacted results (Bandura, 1997), John Hattie (2015) researched influences on student achievement. This research is based on the synthesis of 1,200 meta-analyses on the impacts of student learning outcomes. He found that teacher collective efficacy had one of the most significant effect sizes on student outcomes. So, the goal is not just to get teachers to believe in themselves but also to get teachers to believe in each other.

In order to achieve collective self-efficacy, one must first have belief in oneself. Think back to the staff of 150 teachers and the 4 cycles of PD. Each teacher will eventually reach that goal if the 4 cycles of PD are relevant, timely, and consistent. In the PLCs, teachers will not only learn from one another but they will also be motivated to create change in their classrooms. In addition to providing learning opportunities for teachers, PLCs also share the workload among teachers. In doing so, the PLCs shift the conversation from the individual teacher to the team of teachers, from "I" to "We." This unity creates the collectivism needed to establish collective self-efficacy.

What leadership skills are needed to establish this collective self-efficacy? Again, different leadership skills are needed when building capacity and leadership within a school. Once collective self-efficacy is built in a school, teachers will take their development further than expected. They are then fully motivated. Think about the actual examples in Table 2.3 below from the high school previously discussed.

Teacher Leadership

First, one must understand that no leader can help develop collective self-efficacy without building teacher capacity, i.e., teacher leadership. "One of the most valuable assumptions a principal can grasp and fully embrace is

TABLE 2.3 Examples of Leadership Skills Utilized in Building Collective Self-Efficacy

Leadership	Scenario
Participative leadership	Teachers help decide what PLC forms look like and how they are submitted.
	Teachers help develop the PD plan for the year.
	Teachers help write the strategic plan addressing all content areas.
	Teachers leaders help analyze all data points with administration.
Distributed	Teachers present the data and the basis for the need for the PD plan.
	Teachers help teach PD based on expertise for new teachers, all teachers, and focus groups.
	Teachers conduct research in teams on best practices to incorporate in PD.
	Teachers evaluate PD and make adjustments based on teacher feedback and implantation feedback.
Transformative leadership	School leader presents data and celebrates milestones of success.
	School leader taps teacher leaders to chair school improvement, leadership teams, etc.
	School leader budgets for support of the strategic plan developed by teachers and is transparent about expenditures.

that the job of the principalship is bigger than any one person. One person cannot do it alone, at least not effectively" (Westberry, 2020, p. 126).

Teacher leaders not only support school work but also motivate others to achieve. The old saying that students can teach other students best is true for teachers.

The first step in the teacher leadership quest is conducting a needs assessment. In fact, a needs assessment is the starting point for many initiatives and systems. What leadership abilities exist on staff? What work needs to be done, and how does the information flow? These are critical questions to ask when designing an effective teacher leadership system. Consider the organizational map of a school and devise a leadership map in the same fashion. See Figure 2.2 for an example of a leadership map.

In the example below, the school leader also considers the flow of information. The leaders designed the system so that the school's work can be done effectively with distributive and participatory leadership. All information flows back to the school administration and the leadership team so decisions can be made jointly. For example, the Lead Teachers and the Data Teams report an issue up the chain, and the Best Practices Group conducts the research surrounding that issue. Multiple suggestions and

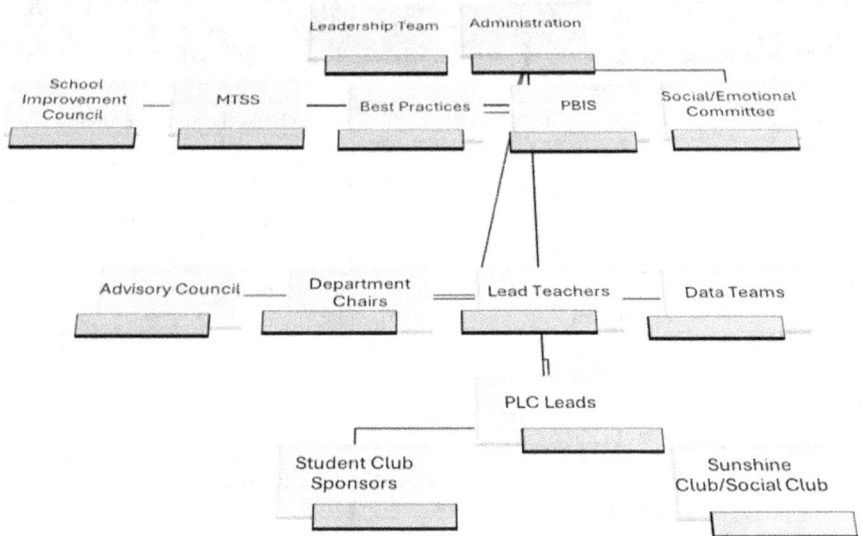

Figure 2.2 Sample leadership map.

proposed solutions are researched and shared with the principal and leadership team for action. Once a decision is made, that information is shared with the Best Practices Group and the School Improvement Council, making it to the Department Chairs and Lead Teachers. Documentation flow must be consistent so that teachers hear the same message. Communication is clear and concise, and school issues are addressed through teacher leadership venues.

This type of distributive leadership model is also transformational. According to Khorshid and Pashazadeh (2014), a transformational leader mobilizes the organization's members to make changes to reach higher performance levels. This type of teacher leadership model, coupled with a system of instructional supervision and applied differentiated leadership skills, also helps to build that collective self-efficacy, which then turns into a culture of a growth mindset, the belief that our abilities can be further developed (Dweck, 2007).

Growth Mindset

Today, leaders in all industries are fixated on developing a growth mindset. Carol Dweck (2007) posits how our beliefs about our abilities can influence our decisions. If one possesses a growth mindset, that person can continue to grow, learn, and evolve. If one has a fixed mindset, that person is less likely to improve performance indicators. That said, a growth mindset is undoubtedly needed in schools, as educators must continue to learn and grow for the sake of the constantly evolving students. Not only do teachers have to possess a growth mindset, but so do administrators. The only way to create a culture of a growth mindset and collective self-efficacy is to provide the system for that learning with and from one another.

Too often, one can find schools that seemingly perform well due to their test score averages. However, if you disaggregate the data, you likely will find that there are subgroups that are vastly underperforming their peers. This achievement gap exists in most schools. For this reason, no one school can afford to maintain the status quo. Educators must always be willing to grow and learn for the sake of all students.

Teacher leadership without a strong system of instructional supervision helps to complete tasks. Teacher leadership with a strong system of instructional supervision, including the four cycles of PD, creates growth. When teachers start seeing results and are celebrated for them, they are motivated to do more.

One of the proudest moments this educator has ever experienced was when the district held town halls to find out what the teachers and parents wanted in their next principal, as this educator then moved to the district level. One teacher, who used to be a sailboat with winds stalled, loudly proclaimed, "We want someone who is going to push us to learn and grow so that we can remain the best in the district!" For someone who was previously content to maintain the status quo to say that was a proud moment.

PRACTICAL GUIDELINES

1. One leadership style does not fit all. Learn about the different leadership styles and when to use each. It would be best to adapt to the needs of the people you are trying to lead and differentiate your leadership skills.
2. Identify teachers' stages of concern and apply the leadership skills needed to advance teachers to the impact stage.
3. Identify which category teachers belong in and make sure you wrap services around your sailboats. This removes the audience for the Uboats, and they need an audience to survive.
4. Develop a systemic instructional supervision plan and consistently implement the plan. This includes all four cycles of PD that must run concurrently to create teacher self-efficacy.
5. To develop a growth mindset in schools, no matter the size of the school, school leaders have to provide the support needed for each teacher at every stage of concern, and teacher leadership is a large component of this system.

CONCLUSION

A plethora of research on leadership skills exists, but school leaders must understand that they must differentiate their leadership styles to fit the needs of the people they are trying to lead. The stages of concern present preface individual needs, and teachers can vacillate from survival to impact during one school year. Therefore, each teacher's leadership skills must differ in order to create self-efficacy. Collective self-efficacy can be achieved through a systemic, well-planned instructional supervision plan incorporating teacher leadership. Teacher leadership is critical in developing a growth mindset in schools. This leadership must be planned and systemic so that teachers, no matter their category or stage of concern, know that together, they can make a difference in students' lives.

CASE STUDY

Ms. Jennifer, the 1st year teacher, was floundering. When invited to her data meeting with the principal, she panicked and suffered anxiety over the questions that would be asked of her. During the conference, Ms. Jennifer stumbled over her answers and tried to present herself as knowledgeable. After the data conference, the principal was unsure about inviting the teacher back for a second year of service, knowing that 1st-year teachers do not have any due process rights. Furthermore, Ms. Jennifer was questioning if she should even teach. To help make the decision, the principal approached Ms. Jennifer's PLC team members and asked about her contributions in the PLC. The principal then discovered that Ms. Jennifer was not attending her PLC regularly and minimally participating. The principal asked Ms. Leslie, a lead teacher and PLC Lead, to assist Ms. Jennifer in her planning and coach her on using data to inform instruction in the classroom. Ms. Leslie was excited to use her coaching skills and mentor a team member, knowing the team is only as strong as its weakest link. After learning about Ms. Jennifer's shortcomings, the principal met with Ms. Jennifer to discuss her concerns.

During this conference, the principal utilized a direct approach to leadership and instructed Ms. Jennifer to attend and contribute to her weekly PLC meetings, work with Ms. Leslie on planning her lessons and assessments, and write a weekly reflection on what she learned. These were non-negotiables that were part of her improvement plan. At the end of the quarter, the principal and Ms. Jennifer were to meet again to discuss any progress or concerns.

At the next meeting, Ms. Jennifer came prepared. The principal opened the conversation by asking Ms. Jennifer to describe her planning process and teaching experiences. Ms. Jennifer talked for 45 minutes without interruption and expressed enthusiasm about her students' growth in a short period. She was proud of the differentiation strategies employed in her classroom and the student engagement. She also communicated how she had successfully built relationships with her students.

She explained her plans for the next steps for her students, which required many next steps for herself. She spoke of her PLC with admiration and how the teachers shared the work and relied on one another; the PLC also provided a springboard for new ideas, which excited Ms. Jennifer. Talk of the new learning management system was mentioned in the PLC, and Ms. Jennifer articulated that she volunteered to teach her PLC team how to use it effectively. It seems Ms. Jennifer is quite proficient in the use of technology. The principal just smiled and congratulated Ms. Jennifer on officially becoming a teacher.

REFLECTIONS ON THE CASE

- What leadership styles are demonstrated in this case? How were they effective for both Ms. Jennifer and Ms. Leslie?
- Describe Ms. Jennifer's stages of concern and how they changed. Is this type of change seen in your school? If so, provide an example.
- Can you provide examples or models of leaders you know who have led transformational change? Describe challenges encountered and/or successes, including the impact on collective self-efficacy and developing a growth mindset.

REFERENCES

Avolio, B., Waldman, D., & Yammarino, F. (1991). The four I's of transformational leadership. *Journal of European Industrial Training, 15*(4), 9–16.

Bandura, A. (1977). Self-efficacy: Toward a unifying theory of behavioral change. *Psychological Review, 84*(2), 191–215.

Bandura, A. (1986). *Social foundations of thought and action: A social cognitive theory.* Prentice Hall.

Bandura, A. (1991). Social cognitive theory of self-regulation. *Organizational Behavior and Human Decision Processes, 50*(2), 248–287.

Bandura, A. (1997). *Self-efficacy: The exercise of control.* Freeman Press.

Bartol, K., & Martin, D. (1994). *Management* (2nd ed). McGraw-Hill.

Bass, B., & Avolio, B. (1993). Transformational leadership and organizational culture. *Public Administration Quarterly, 17*(1), 112–121.

Burns, J. M. (1978). *Leadership.* HarperCollins.

Donohoo, J., Hattie, J., & Eells, R. (2018). The power of collective efficacy. *Educational Leadership, 75*(6), 40–44.

Dweck, C. (2007). *Mindset: The new psychology of success.* Ballantine Books.

Fuller, F. F. (1969). Concerns of teachers: A developmental conceptualization. *American Educational Research Journal, 6,* 207–226.

Gibb, C. A. (1954). Leadership. In G. Lindzey (Ed.), *Handbook of social psychology* (Vol. 2, pp. 877–917). Addison-Wesley.

Glickman, C., Gordon, S., & Gordon, J. (2017). *Supervision and instructional leadership: A developmental approach.* Pearson Education.

Greenleaf, R. K. (2003). *The servant-leader within: A transformative path.* Paulist Press.

Hattie, J. (2015). The applicability of visible learning to higher education. *Scholarship of Teaching and Learning in Psychology, 1*(1), 79–91. https://doi.org/10.1037/stl0000021

Hattie, J. A. C., & Zierer, K. (2018). *Ten mindframes for visible learning: Teaching for success.* Routledge.

Khorshid, S., & Pashazadeh, A. (2014). The effect of transformational leadership on organizational learning capabilities with respect to the mediating role of organizational intelligence. *Journal of Change Management, 6*(11), 7.

Lee, C., & Bobko, P. (1994). Self-efficacy beliefs: Comparison of five measures. *Journal of Applied Psychology, 79*(3), 364–369.

Leithwood, K., & Jantzi, D. (2006). Transformational school leadership for large-scale reform: Effects on students, teachers, and their classroom practices. *School Effectiveness and School Improvement, 17*(2), 201–227. https://doi.org/10.1080/09243450600565829

Lessing, C. & De Witt, M. (2007). The value of continuous professional development: Teachers' perceptions. *South African Journal of Education, 27*(1), 53–67.

Lewis, C. (2009). What is the nature of knowledge development in lesson study? *Educational Action Research, 17*(1), 95–110.

Likert, R. (1961). *New patterns of management.* McGraw-Hill.

Robbins, S., Judge, T., & Sanghai, S. (2007). *Organizational behavior* (12th ed.). Pearson.

Tygret, J. A. (2018). The preparation and education of first-year teachers: A case study. *The Qualitative Report, 23*(3), 710–729.

Westberry, L. (2020). *Putting the pieces together: A systems approach to school leadership.* Rowman and Littlefield.

Yeager, D. S., & Dweck, C. S. (2020). What can be learned from growth mindset controversies? *American Psychologist, 75*(9), 1269–1284. https://doi.org/10.1037/amp0000794

Zepeda, S. (2018). *Instructional supervision: Applying tools and concepts.* Routledge.

CHAPTER 3

LEADING CHANGE TO IMPROVE THE PROFESSIONAL DEVELOPMENT OF ISRAELI TEACHERS

Michael Reichel
Michlalah Jerusalem College, Israel

Shmuel Shenhav
Michlalah Jerusalem College, Israel

Daniel Chester
Michlalah Jerusalem College, Israel

Shoshana Karlinsky
Ministry of Education, Israel

ABSTRACT

Chapter 3 contributors, Drs. Reichel and Shenhav, along with Research Lecturer Daniel Chester and a recent master's graduate student Shoshana Karlinsky, report on a mixed-methods study analyzing the results of a questionnaire distributed to 217 school leaders (teachers and principals) to assess the state of teacher professional development (PD). Interviews were also conducted with 20 school principals. PD, in many schools, is episodic, often administered in a top-down fashion initiated without meaningful input by teachers, among other problems. The study conducted by the chapter authors reflects several intractable issues in offering effective PD. The discussion focuses on the importance of transformational and instructional leadership to make PD more effective on several levels. Concrete suggestions for doing so are proffered.

Keywords: Professional development; instructional leaders; effective teaching; teacher training; cultural change; visionary leadership

---

Prefocus Guiding Questions

- *A principal comments, "I hire the best and leave them be. They don't need additional professional development (PD) activities." How might you respond to such a statement?*
- *How effective have the PD sessions you have taken as an educator been? Explain why they were effective or not.*
- *What recommendations do you have for improving PD for teachers?*

INTRODUCTION

PD is ubiquitous. Most school systems require teachers to undertake a designated number of hours of PD throughout their tenure (Sancar et al., 2021). Recent research indicates the dubious value of much of the PD offered to teachers (Korthagen & Nuijten, 2022). In their classic work on PD, Darling-Hammond and colleagues (2009) critiqued extant PD and pointed to much-needed reforms.

The theoretical framework draws on the literature of transformational leadership that has received much attention in educational leadership literature (e.g., Ahmad et al., 2020). Although other theorists have historically examined transformational leadership (e.g., Bass, 1997; Burns, 1978; House, 1976), Leithwood and Jantzi (2005) addressed the implications of transformational leadership for schools. According to them, "three broad categories of leadership practices" could be identified: setting directions, developing people, and redesigning the organization. The authors explained that setting directions is a "critical aspect of transformational leadership ... [by] ... helping staff to develop shared understandings about the school and its activities as well as the goals that undergird a sense of purpose or vision" (pp. 38–39). They explained that people are more likely to participate when they have had a say in developing ideas and practices. Transformational leaders realize that anyone can set a direction for an organization. However, it is the effective leader who considers and solicits the participation of other key school personnel to share in the development and actualization of the institutional vision and purpose.

The chapter reports on a mixed methods study analyzing the results of a questionnaire distributed to 217 Israeli school leaders (teachers and principals) to assess the state of teacher professional development (TPD). Interviews were conducted with 20 school principals and a group focus with 20 teachers. The change process is discussed by drawing from the literature on transformational school change. Suggestions for making PD more effective are discussed.

LITERATURE REVIEW

This literature review aims to determine the role of school leaders in promoting TPD. Three main themes will be reviewed when exploring different aspects of school leaders' impact on teachers' attitudes toward PD.

- The first theme will discuss the advantages of TPD and how professionalism may be achieved.
- The second theme will discuss key components for creating meaningful and effective TPD.
- The third theme will focus on school leaders' approaches and attitudes toward TPD and review how different school leaders promote it.

Professional Development for Israeli Teachers

TPD in Israel is optional, as will be noted below. When it does occur, it is provided at school (*Hishtalmut Beit Sifrit*), which is formed and designed to meet the specific needs of the school staff. Face-to-face learning outside the school usually occurs at a regional *Mercaz Pisga*, a teacher-learning center run by the Ministry of Education. Teachers who participate in a PD of a 112-hour in-service course (*Hishtalmut*) and complete an assignment are eligible for a *Gmul Hishtalmut*. This PD credit is an additional payment of 1.2% to the gross monthly payment. Teachers may be paid up to 18 *Gmulim* throughout their teaching careers. In-service courses may be synchronous, asynchronous, or hybrid (Hozer Mankal, 2006).

PD is defined as teacher learning (Ackah-Jnr, 2020). Darling-Hammond and colleagues (2017) define PD as teacher-structured learning that changes teaching practices and improves students' achievements. TPD also refers to teachers' ability to learn how to learn and to apply their knowledge in practice to support their students' learning.

Avidav-Unger (2024) elaborates on the definition of TPD. Avidav-Unger explains that PD occurs throughout a teacher's career and is a "lifelong learning." PD is not merely a process affecting teachers' understanding of knowledge, methodologies, and pedagogy. It should lead to creating teachers' professional and organizational profiles and empowering teachers' abilities. Such learning may affect teachers positively, as they can lead and make changes. PD helps teachers become innovative, creative, and productive.

The literature indicates that the content of PD for teachers must prioritize the teacher's needs to improve student learning outcomes. In the 21st century, PD has become even more crucial than before. Increasing numbers of school leaders have become aware that teachers' skill sets and toolboxes are changing rapidly. Teaching in a world of stability, certainty, simplicity, and clarity is replaced by extremely different learning conditions. Practices, methods, and bodies of knowledge keep changing daily. Artificial Intelligence, for instance, is impacting all aspects of life. Artificial Intelligence in Education, has raised challenging issues and ethical concerns, such as fairness, accountability, transparency, autonomy, and more (Holmes et al., 2022).

It has become clear that TPD needs to be relevant and advanced to improve student performance. Today, students need skills way beyond the skills of the past. PD has to be such that it addresses the requirements of this time and age. The call now is for teachers who are professionally developed and are VUCA learners (Hadar et al., 2020). Those teachers keep their professional development learning non-stop; they understand how to teach, especially in times of *v*olatility, *u*ncertainty, *c*omplexity, and *a*mbiguity. Most importantly, they view the VUCA world as a catalyst rather than a barrier blocking the way to success. Teachers who do not keep themselves constantly updated may find themselves, sooner or later, outdated, unqualified, and unemployed.

In summary, there is ample evidence to suggest that teacher learning has a significant impact on teachers' knowledge, as well as the performance of their students. When well-designed and effectively implemented, PD can improve student outcomes (Darling-Hammond et al., 2017). Recent research has demonstrated a positive correlation between student achievement and teacher attendance in professional development programs (Krasniqi, 2021). Based on existing literature, the school leader's primary responsibility is to recognize the crucial role of teacher learning in shaping the success of both students and teachers.

Essential Elements for Effective TPD

Successful PD improves students' academic achievements and promotes the school's goals (Bredeson, 2000; Postholm, 2012). The literature recognizes the importance of PD as life-long learning to the teacher's career and personality, the student's success, and the school's success. The framework for effective PD is widely discussed in the literature. Key components include (Desimone & Garet, 2015):

- Focusing on content: Activities involving subject matter content and how students learn that content.
- Active learning: Opportunities for peer observation and peer learning, analyzing students' work, discussing case studies, sharing experiences, and creating learning materials rather than passively listening to lectures.
- Coherence: Content, objectives, methods, and practices that support the school curriculum and the needs of the teachers and the students so that the learning process can occur.
- Sustained duration: An ongoing process that lasts throughout the school year, allowing teachers to move from theory to practice, implement, get feedback, and reflect on their learning.
- Collective participation: Groups of teachers from the same school, subject, or grade form professional interactive learning communities.
- Personalized content: This allows teachers to choose the content according to their own needs and provides learning experiences to meet those needs.
- Convenience: School-based and embedded in teacher's daily work.
- Applicability: Creating opportunities in which teachers tie the theory with instructive practices.

In addition to traditional TPD, Macià and García (2016) revealed that teachers who participate in informal PD involving peer observations, group work, and new technologies are key factors in improving students' performance. Such learning may occur in professional learning communities (PLCs). A PLC is formed by a group of teachers and school leaders who collaboratively examine and discuss different teaching practices and, as a result, develop unique methods and ideas to manage the typical issues and challenges they face at school. PLCs are highly recommended as successful teacher-learning programs (Johnson & Voelkel, 2019). PLCs have a few dimensions. When followed, they turn into effective and successful PD opportunities:

- The facilitator shares leadership and support equally with the teachers
- All of the group members share a common vision and mission
- School leaders and teachers learn collectively and collaboratively
- Learning resources are equal for both school leaders and teachers
- Peer review, peer learning, reflection, and feedback performed by teachers and school leaders alike (Glanz, 2024).

Understanding the essentials of effective PD may assist school leaders in choosing the best opportunities for their staff and students. Moreover, PLCs value teachers' professionalism by creating a learning environment among staff and principals.

Attitudes and Approaches of School Leaders Toward PD

For effective PD to occur, the cooperation and action of school leaders are expected. One act school leaders can take is to support teacher learning and provide a learning environment for teachers and not only students (Krasniqi, 2021). Teachers who work in a supportive learning environment improve their effectiveness (Kraft & Papay, 2014).

In-service courses in or outside school are beneficial for teacher excellence. However, regular discussions between teachers and principals can achieve even better outcomes regarding instructional practices or content. Professional principals or school leaders knowledgeable about appropriate teaching and learning practices are a tremendous source of knowledge available and accessible to teachers, compared to episodic and generic professional development courses. School leaders who frequently engage in pedagogical, educational, or ethical discussions with teachers can create a learning environment that promotes self-awareness and improvement in teaching practices. This ongoing process is an important aspect of the school leader's role as an "instructional supervisor." A school leader who functions as an instructional supervisor affects teachers' performance significantly. True supervision supports and enhances school teacher learning (Glanz, 2024).

Engaging in such discussions improves teaching skills but lacks the advantage of participating in a course with 12–40 other teachers. Therefore, school principals should also provide their teachers with learning opportunities by designing and encouraging participation in in-service PD courses. According to Darling-Hammond et al. (2017), school leaders should not only design PD that meets the requirements listed above to become effective, but they should also make adaptions of existing teacher learning programs to suit teachers' needs, such as identifying and developing expert teachers as mentors and coaches to support learning in the particular areas of expertise of other teachers.

The school leader's role is to provide teachers with adequate programs and learning experiences. In addition, for professional development to affect teachers' performance and students' achievements, school leaders should follow the learning process, ensuring teachers practice the knowledge and skills learned within the professional development framework.

Promoting teachers' learning in school may also affect the principal's leadership approach. School principals who promote and implement teacher learning may face teachers' resistance. Teachers often find professional development short-term, episodic, and disconnected from their professional skill sets and interests (DeMonte, 2013). Other reasons might be the new reforms, which result in longer teaching days at school, and generic PD programs in which teachers must participate (*Hozer Mankal*, 2006). As a result, school leaders are faced with resistance to participating in PD programs. Different instructional leadership approaches should be applied in such cases; directive, collaborative, and self-directed approaches help principals create a teacher-learning culture in their schools (Sullivan & Glanz, 2013). Principals have the lead role in this process and must make decisions to ensure collaboration amongst the school staff (Krasniqi, 2021).

The literature emphasizes the importance of PD for teachers. Teachers who learn new methods and examine their teaching practices and teachers who use the wisdom of colleagues and experts around them to improve their teaching habits become professionals. Professionalism in education usually results in better student performance. School leaders who follow the Ministry of Education regulations for PD allow their teachers to benefit from additional advantages beyond improved skills, as they can also provide financial benefits.

Much thought is needed to introduce or design PD courses for teachers. Based on research, the literature focuses on a few components that are the key to successful teacher learning. Integrating those components in any in-service course for teachers may transform it into a beneficial, meaningful, applicable, and stimulating learning experience.

The principal plays a significant role in promoting TPD. Reviewing content, applying varied leadership approaches, implementing new practices, creating a learning environment, and engaging in pedagogical–educational discussions with teachers are all fundamental actions that encourage and motivate teachers' learning.

Transforming School Culture that Supports Effective PD

As indicated at the outset of this chapter, many PD efforts are ineffective, as borne out partly in our study that follows. If we support the obvious notion that everyone can benefit enormously from PD, then the issue is how best to frame the school's culture to support ongoing learning for teachers. An understanding of the change process is crucial.

Much of the recent literature on school change emerged from the work of Michael Fullan's (2008) "key drivers for change" in his discussion of "change knowledge." It should be noted that his work is rooted in the groundbreaking work done decades earlier by Seymour Sarason (1982) in his *The Culture of the School and the Problem of Change*. Sarason posited that change occurs most fundamentally by addressing a school's culture, i.e., the beliefs and actions of stakeholders about teaching and learning. Otherwise, change is ephemeral and ineffective.

Fullan, Sarason, and others argue that change is inevitable because of the ever-increasing complexity of a school's diverse environment. Educators in the 21st century confront a plethora of challenges. For example, there are more students than ever identified with emotional and learning issues (because our diagnostic tools and awareness have improved); communal pressures that compel school leaders to remain responsive to a growing, varied, and diverse constituency are ever-present; technological innovations (especially with the advent of artificial intelligence) affect the nature of learning and teaching; the political and social landscape has been affected, more than ever in recent times, by polarized vested interests, etc. These internal and external vicissitudes inevitably challenge school leaders' convictions and intestinal fortitude. Because problems are more intractable today, educators have relied on a theory of leadership to guide their work in schools. Transformational school leadership theory provides foundational guidance for school leaders.

A transformational visionary agenda includes a redesign or, at the very least, a reexamination of a school's commitment to teacher quality, teacher growth, instructional excellence, and student learning. Although no theory of leadership is without criticism, transformational leadership informs the work of school leaders. These leaders who want to transform the culture of their schools champion a vision of instructional excellence that includes best practices in PD.

Transformational leaders work to alter school culture by nurturing a PLC (Pan & Cheng, 2023). They serve as change agents or facilitators to actualize their vision for instructional excellence (Fullan, 2006; Rush, 2022). They work diligently and consistently to keep instructional quality as their main focus.

Transforming schools is easy if done superficially. Such change, however, is ephemeral. Unfortunately, Fullan (2003) says much change occurs at this superficial level. He says that much of the change in schools in the 1960s around innovative instructional and curricular practices was short-lived because they were implemented on the surface without a deep change in people's beliefs and behavior. Both Fullan (2003) and Starratt (1995) concur that change without addressing a change in core beliefs and values is doomed to remain temporary and superficial. "Transformational leadership," says Starratt (1995), "is concerned with large, collective values ..." (p. 110). Leadership is predicated on the foundation of changing core beliefs and values.

Michael Fullan (1991, cited by Fullan, 2003) has identified

> ...five crucial mind and action sets that leaders in the 21st century must cultivate: a deep sense of moral purpose, knowledge of the change process,

capacity to develop relationships across diverse individuals and groups, skills in fostering knowledge creation and sharing, and the ability to engage with others in coherence making amidst multiple innovations. (p. 35)

1. Engaging people's moral purposes: School leaders do a good job of setting the vision for students' social, emotional, and academic growth. Embedded in such a vision is a detailed articulation of the school's commitment to instructional excellence for all students. A school leader with such a vision is committed to refining the lives of children by improving the quality of the instruction they receive. Such a commitment is predicated on serving the needs of all students within an inclusive learning environment while remaining cognizant of extant research into the latest and most effective teaching pedagogies.
2. Understand the change process: Although Fullan discusses several ideas about change, we will highlight some relevant ones. According to Fullan, the "implementation dip" is a proverbial landmine. People, often board members, expect fast results. Fullan says, "Since change involves grappling with new beliefs and understandings, and new skills, competencies, and behaviors, it is inevitable that it will not go smoothly in the early stages of implementation." Such an understanding helps people within the organization to relax and experiment with new ideas, practices, and policies. Learning anything new is initially "awkward." Furthermore, awareness of this "implementation dip" shortens the dip, according to Fullan. Another aspect of change, for Fullan, is the realization of the necessity to overcome fear. Citing research by Black and Gregersen (2002 as cited by Fullan, 2006), Fullan explains why people seem immobilized despite a clear vision. He cites Black and Gregersen's answer: "The clearer the new vision, the easier it is for people to see all the specific ways they will be incompetent and look stupid. Many prefer to be competent at the [old] wrong thing than incompetent at the [new] right thing" (p. 69).
3. Cultures for Learning: According to Fullan, this third mindset of change encourages establishing a conducive environment "so that people can learn from each other and become collectively committed to improvement." That is why involving teachers in decision-making about curriculum and instruction is so critical. Mechanisms and structures within a school need to be developed to allow for and facilitate communication among teachers and administrators about instruction. Instructional conversations, whether they take the form of lesson studies among members of the math department, "critical friends" teacher groups, action research projects by individual teachers, or supervisory strategies that encourage

instructional dialogue about the proper use of wait time, are at the heart of a professional learning community that values instructional improvement.
4. Cultures of Evaluation: Coupled with these emphases on instructional improvement is a focus on assessment. Gathering data on student learning continuously in aggregated and disaggregated ways and developing action plans based on an analysis of the data from parent, teacher, and student satisfaction surveys in order to inform instructional decision-making are examples of creating a culture of evaluation or assessment in a school. Fullan explains, "When schools ... increase their collective capacity to engage in ongoing assessment for learning, major improvements are achieved." Citing Jim Collins (2002 cited by Fullan, 2007), he explains that "great organizations" have a "commitment to 'confronting the brutal facts' and establishing a culture of disciplined inquiry."
5. Leadership for change: Fullan asks, "What is the best leadership style for effecting the changes that are necessary in schools?" He explains, "It turns out that high-flying, charismatic leaders look like powerful change agents but are bad for business because too much revolves around themselves." Leadership, he continues, must be distributed throughout the organization.

In applying Fullan's work, school leaders need a moral commitment to follow through on the change initiatives. They need to ensure that teaching is more student-engaging with cycles of checking for understanding and feedback. The use of more formative assessments is necessary. School leaders must involve teachers in curriculum development and the kind of PD best suited for them. They need to be conversant with alternatives to traditional supervision. Seeking ways to make teacher evaluation more effective to encourage teachers to improve their practice should be high on their agenda.

School leaders need the moral imperative to remain committed to instructional excellence by offering insights into ways our work in instruction can enhance teachers' dignity, impact student learning, transform their work, and, in the process, transform schools themselves so that taken-for-granted educational practices turn into new opportunities and stagnation into transformation.

METHODS

This mixed-methods study drew on data collected between the spring and fall semesters of 2022 from teachers and principals from all over Israel, primarily in the Central sections of the country. Study participants were informed of the study's purpose and that they would voluntarily complete a 20-item questionnaire to assess the nature and quality of PD in their schools. Their responses would be reported so as not to identify them. Those interviewed individually or in a group were given the same information, including privacy notice. Data were collected via Google Forms and tabulated using descriptive statistics.

Context of the Study

The current study focused on Israeli school principals and teachers. The national school system in Israel serves about 1.6 million students, with approximately 73% in the Jewish sector and 27% in the Arab sector (Israeli Ministry of Education, 2020). Mindful of the diversity among school populations, recent educational policy in Israel has been directed toward achieving high levels of equality in educational outcomes across the board, thus aiming to narrow the achievement gap upward through growing performance pressure. In practice, however, Israeli student achievements are still characterized by a rising achievement gap, as evidenced in various international comparative examination studies (BenDavid-Hadar, 2016).

The primary role of Israeli school principals and the supervisory support team as articulated by Capstones, the institute that spearheads school principals' development in Israel, is to serve as instructional leaders to improve all students' education and learning (Capstones, 2008). Four additional areas of management support this function: designing the school's future image—developing a vision and bringing about change; leading the staff and nurturing its professional development; focusing on the individual; and managing the relationship between the school and the surrounding community (Capstones, 2008).

Understanding the unique context and background of how PD is offered in Israel is also essential. PD is needed, albeit not required, for teachers to receive a salary increase. To receive an increase, teachers must participate over three years for a certain amount of continued education and PD. The range of required hours is between 30 and 60 hours. Courses taken as part of a master's degree program cannot be counted toward PD because teachers receive a 6 and 10% salary increase. PD is separate. A teacher's salary is determined by their years of experience, degrees, and amount of PD hours taken.

Principals cannot require teachers to undertake PD; although many get that remuneration raise, it is voluntary. If a principal conducts an in-service PD session for teachers, they do not have to attend. The principal does not have the authority to require specific teachers to take specific courses but rather must encourage the staff to agree to participate or follow the principal's direction in participating in the school's PD or attending other non-school related PD workshops. Most Israeli teachers, however, take PD.

Sample and Data Collection

This study, related to the questionnaire, included 217 participants (70% teachers and 30% principals). Eighty-six (39.5%) men and 131 (60.4%) women. Concerning the type of schools, 55 (26%) work in ultra-Orthodox schools. 141 (66.8%) in state and religious public state schools, 7 (3.3%) in non-Orthodox public state schools, and 8 (3.8%) in ultra-Orthodox public state schools. In reporting the results of this study for this chapter, we did not differentiate the various types of schools.

The years of seniority of the respondents ranged from one year to 40, with an average of 13.2 years. Sixteen (7.5%) respondents had one to two years of experience. 43 (20.3%) had seniority in their position of 3–5 years, 60 (28.3%) had seniority of 5–10 years, 65 (30.7%) had 10–20 years of experience, and 28 (13.2%) had more than 20 years of experience. Similarly, this study did not report results based on years of experience.

Survey Instruments

After a short 2-item demographic section consisting of participants' type of position and grade level, the second section consisted of a 20-item Likert-Scale questionnaire that measured the degree of agreement with the statements ranging from 1 (not at all) to 4 (very much).

The questionnaire was designed based on extant literature on the nature of PD. Items were randomly assigned to avoid a response set. The questionnaire consisted of three scales with associated reliabilities.

- Involvement of teachers in professional development processes that included seven questions. $\alpha = 0.74$
- Involvement of school principals in the professional development of teachers, which included six questions. $\alpha = 0.69$
- Autonomy of managers in setting policies and professional development plans that included seven questions. $\alpha = 0.56$

The reliability of the general questionnaire was 0.76.

Data Analysis

The instrument attempted to assess teachers' and principals' perceptions and experiences about the nature of PD in their schools and the roles played by study participants. We especially wanted to contrast these school leaders' and classroom teachers' perceptions and experiences.

Our initial research question was:

- What are the perceptions of classroom teachers and principals about the nature and quality of PD?

We then analyzed the results using descriptive statistics and found PD lacking and a discrepancy, in some instances, between teachers' responses compared to those of principals. We then added a second research question:

- How can educational leaders improve instructional practices through targeted educational reforms to improve the delivery and practice of TPD?

This question led us to study the change process, its parameters, and its challenges. We then decided to find a principal and his teachers who attempted to implement changes in PD. After visiting and interviewing the school leaders in one particular school, we created a case study highlighting these instructional (PD) improvement attempts. In doing so, we gained insights about the change process.

Frequency charts for each of the 20 items on the questionnaire were created, demonstrating means, standard deviations, and percentages.

FINDINGS

Given space limitations and the primary focus of this book chapter, we will highlight the main findings, leaving a fuller discussion for an article in the future.

Questionnaire Findings

In answer to the first research question about teachers' and principals' perceptions of the nature and quality of PD, principal respondents acknowledged that it was their responsibility to provide effective PD for teachers. However, teachers reported that PD initiatives were unsatisfactory. For instance, regarding PD (sample item below, Table 3.1), 89% of teacher respondents indicated PD was poorly conducted.

Another striking finding highlighted the lack of teacher involvement and the irrelevance of much PD to the needs of teachers, as reported by teacher respondents. On the other hand, principals did not address teacher involvement as a significant lack in their school's PD program. To evidence the difference between the teaching staff and the management team regarding this issue, the Welch's t-test was performed on the data, and it was found that the average management team ($M = 3.06$, sd = 0.65) was significantly higher than the average of teachers ($M = 2.57$, sd = 0.94)

TABLE 3.1 Professional Development Is an Ongoing Process That Provides a Personal Response to Each Participant and Is Beneficial

	Counts	% of Total	Cumulative %
1	4	1.8%	1.8%
2	22	10.1%	11.9%
3	68	31.2%	43.1%
4	124	56.9%	100.0%

Note: Mean of total responders 3.43 of 4.

TABLE 3.2 Averages and Standard Deviation in Teacher and Staff Engagement in PD

Group	N	Mean	Median	SD	SE
Teachers	175	2.57	3.00	0.949	0.0718
Management	17	3.06	3.00	0.659	0.160

($t(23) = -2.78$, $p < 0.05$). In other words, there was a significant difference in the sense of involvement between the teaching staff and the administrative staff in that the administrative staff felt that the teachers were more involved in the PD processes than reported by the teachers. Table 3.2 shows averages and standard deviations of this finding:

Interviews: Findings Reported by Principals About the Nature and Quality of PD

The interviews indicated that most principals reported that TPD is the principal's responsibility. One representative principal stated, "The responsibility is mine as a manager." Several principals indicated that although they see themselves as "in charge" of PD, in practice, other staff members also lead and implement the PD: "I refer the teachers to continuing education program … But the assistant principal is responsible for it" or "administered by the assistant principal and pedagogical coordinator."

In Israel, schools provide PD regularly, "Usually every few weeks," reported one principal, … but they (teachers) also take workshops of their own choice outside the school." "So," said another principal, "they do have a choice on the kind of PD they want." Still, most principals attested to the fact that they see PD as their primary responsibility in terms of its offering and content. Another representative participant stated, "Principals see the subject of PD as being under their responsibility; they are the ones who determine the subjects offered."

Several other principals admitted that the quality of PD was lacking:

> The PD is helpful, to a small extent, due to the teachers being obliged to attend. If the topic is interesting and relevant, there is a chance of improving the quality of teaching. It does not necessarily contribute to the quality of teaching, ... perhaps partially... There are good training courses, and there are less effective ones. In most cases, it is not possible to predict in advance the quality of the PD courses.

Group Focus Interviews: Findings Reported by Teachers About the Nature and Quality of PD

A group of 20 teachers was interviewed in a group in graduate-level class at Michlala Jerusalem College in May 2024 about their attitudes toward their PD experiences. They reported that PD was mandated by the Ministry and principal at the particular school, but they had little or no say about its content. "We are told there's going to be PD next week on technology. I was not asked if I needed such PD. I was mandated to attend," reported one study participant. Others echoed the same sentiment. One stark comment was representative:

> The vast majority of principals do not include us in deciding what topics are will be chosen for PD. The principal and the other administrators usually make the decision.

About five teachers reported, "My school offers no in-house PD. I'm expected to go elsewhere on my own."

On the positive side, several teachers reported that the PD offered "are usually interesting," even though they have no choice in its selection at the school level. One teacher said, "They try to bring speakers to teach us new skills for classroom teaching."

None of those who participated in the Group Focus stated that there was follow-up practice with feedback on any PD workshops offered. Some did appreciate "the comradery among the teachers at these meetings."

IMPROVING PD IN ISRAEL

This chapter section offers suggestions in response to the second research question, "How can educational leaders improve instructional practices through targeted educational reforms to improve the delivery and practice of TPD?" Although the study involves Israeli educators, we believe the suggestions apply to many teachers in various schools almost anywhere.

The first set of suggestions is drawn primarily on reports from principals, primarily from the interviews in this study:

- Teachers need a voice in the type of PD offered. However, the primary responsibility for PD topics should be assigned to a committee representing management with some teacher representatives.
- PD should be mandated without allowing teachers to opt out. Teachers of all levels of experience should experience PD.
- Principals should meet with each teacher for an annual review to mutually determine the best PD for that particular teacher. Hence, the study participants suggested that PD should be differentiated. Not all teachers need the same topics covered in PD.
- Principals agreed that a change in culture about the importance of PD is necessary. Some principals weren't certain that the Ministry of Education was committed enough to allocate much-needed additional funds to support PD. A few principals questioned the need for PD, although most affirmed its importance. Almost all agreed that teachers should be required to attend PD. A recurring theme revolved around exposing teachers to PD that they deemed of value. "Some teachers reluctantly attend workshops unrelated to their needs or interests simply because they want to accumulate the requisite hours to receive the extra stipends offered."

The second set of suggestions is drawn primarily on reports from teachers, primarily from the group focus interviews in this study:

- Teachers reported that they should have more input and decision-making authority to determine PD's nature, type, and frequency.
- They also posited that additional funds should be available to remunerate teachers to attend PD opportunities.
- Teachers for whom PD is necessary should have a majority say regarding PD topics.

LEADING CHANGE TO IMPROVE PD

The following general suggestions are offered based on the change literature briefly reported earlier in this chapter.

- Educational leaders should first realize that current efforts in offering PD are inadequate and need reform.
- Realize that resistance to change is common and should be expected.

- Success is a multi-layered, gradual process that is not always assured, but improvements, even incremental ones, occur.
- Implement new changes slowly (even one at a time) and provide participants enough time to fully understand expectations and time to build requisite skills to ensure success.
- Give faculty real opportunities to recommend policy changes, e.g., topics for PD.
- Changing and building a new culture of learning and improvement takes time and continuous commitment. Positive instructional change in any school is inevitably fraught with challenges, including resistance and ambivalence. Renewal can occur in time. The school is still in the process of developing new ways of learning and improving.
- Schools with "permeable connectivity" successfully accomplish meaningful change (Fullan, 2006).
- Principals who provide sufficient financial support and otherwise are best at sustaining faculty interest in the specific reform.

Several criteria are also included based on extant literature on best practices in PD to guide educational leaders in creating the most effective PD program possible.

PD is among the most powerful ways to enhance and improve the knowledge and skills of educators (Popova et al., 2021). Unfortunately, the way in which PD is introduced and practiced is flawed.

Teachers have not been involved in planning the kind of PD they need. Other issues abound as well. The PD group decided to explore PD as best practice in these ways:

- Purposeful and articulated—Goals for a PD program must be developed, examined, critiqued, and assessed for relevance.
- Participatory and collaborative—PD is often top-driven, even by administrative fiat. Such programs are less effective because teachers for whom PD serves the greatest benefit are not actively involved in its design, implementation, and assessment. Best practice in PD requires wide participation by all stakeholders.
- Knowledge-based and discipline-based—PD must be based on the most relevant and current research in the field. Also, teachers will not value PD unless it contains, in the words of one teacher, "some substance, ... something I can take back to the classroom."
- Focused on student learning—According to Lindstrom and Speck (2004), "Educators must never forget that the objective of professional development is to increase student learning" (p. 156). PD programs should consider teacher behaviors or activities that directly

impact student learning and then "work backward to pinpoint the knowledge, skills, and attitudes educators must have" (p. 157).
- Ongoing—Too much PD is of the one-shot variety. For instance, a leader delivers a workshop and then leaves without any follow-up. Such efforts have marginal value at best. PD opportunities must be made available continuously to sustain ideas and practices. PD cannot significantly impact classroom practice unless workshops and programs are continually offered.
- Developmental—PD must not only be ongoing but developmental, i.e., building gradually on teacher knowledge and skills in a given area or topic.
- Analytical and reflective—PD opportunities must promote instructional dialogue and thinking about teaching practice and purposefully address ways of helping students achieve more. Also, PD must be continuously assessed in terms of its relevance and value to teachers.

The latest research findings indicate that PD significantly affects student achievement and requires at least dozens of hours on a given topic (Glanz, 2024; Gore et al., 2021).

CONCLUSION

Changing and building a new PD learning and improvement culture through empowering school leaders takes time and continuous commitment. Schools of the 21st century need leaders who can effectively and efficiently manage the change process. This new breed of principals realizes that leadership and management must be well coordinated as processes and functions. Older notions that bifurcate the two processes are no longer relevant in the 21st century.

PD should be part of the school's multi-year (long-term) strategic effort in which all stakeholders, teachers, principals, and Ministry of Education officials collaborate to offer effective PD. PD is too important. This study evidenced the differences between teachers and principals regarding some aspects of PD. A meeting of the minds in concert with best practices culled from research and literature on PD is necessary.

CASE STUDY

Veroh's Elementary School in Israel is an urban school with 65 teachers and 400 students in grades 1–6. One hundred -percent of the students go on to high school, and ninety-five percent will continue toward college. Among its peers, the school is considered to be academically rigorous. However, it does offer leveled learning experiences for its diverse student body and is known to have a caring administration.

The average years of experience among teachers is 15, with about three new teachers entering each year due to faculty retirements. The school is administered by three individuals, each with a different focus: i.e. general, overall school administration (principal), student support (assistant principal), and a school-community liaison (assistant principal).

The principal wants to transform his instructional program based on discussions and ideas he learned in his second degree in school administration at a local college. He was exposed to the literature on instructional transformation, which utilizes the most current pedagogical and supervisory strategies as well as cutting-edge educational practices.

In one interview, he stated, "Educational quality is achieved to the extent to which those educators who work within the school are empowered to focus on instructional matters. I see my role as empowering my faculty toward instructional excellence." The principal, whom we'll refer to as Mr. Mark, indicated that his teaching staff, especially the more experienced ones, were traditional in applying their pedagogical practices. "Teaching," explained Mr. Mark, "is all too frontal for my liking." Moreover, he explained, "Even my use of PD and supervision is outdated, as I learned during my master's degree program." He also explained that he learned about best practices in PD, which are purposeful and articulated, collaboratively developed, discipline-based, focused on student learning, developmental, analytical, and ongoing. "Our PD has not met any of these criteria. Where am I to begin?"

REFLECTIONS ON THE CASE

- What concrete suggestions can you offer Mr. Mark?
- Even if Mr. Mark were committed to addressing each PD criterion expressed above, how might he gain support from the Ministry of Education, which has traditionally paid little attention to PD?
- Reflecting on the best PD practices mentioned above, to what extent does your school reflect these criteria?

REFERENCES

Ackah-Jnr, F. R. (2020). The teacher should be learning: In-service professional development and learning of teachers implementing inclusive education in early childhood education settings. *International Journal of Whole Schooling, 16*(2), 93–121.

Ahmad, A., Ambad, S., & Mohd, S. (2020). The trend of research on transformational leadership literature: A bibliometric analysis. *International Journal of Human Resource Studies, 11.* https://doi.org/10.5296/ijhrs.v11i1.18074

Avidav-Unger, O. (2024). *The personalized continuing professional learning of teachers: A global perspective.* Routledge.

Bass, B. M. (1997). Does the transactional/transformational leadership transcend organizational and national boundaries? *American Psychologist, 52,* 130–139.

BenDavid-Hadar, I. (2016). School finance policy and social justice. *International Journal of Educational Development, 46,* 166–174.

Bredeson, P. V. (2000). The school principal's role in teacher professional development. *Journal of In-Service Education, 26*(2), 385–401.

Burns, J. M. (1978). *Leadership.* Harper & Row.

Capstones – The Israeli Institute for School Leadership. (2008). *Perception of the principal's role in the state of Israel: Report by the professional committee to formulate policy recommendations for the Ministry of Education.* Avney Rosha.

Darling-Hammond, L., Chung Wei, R., Andrei, A., Richardson, N., & Orphanos, S. (2009). *Professional learning in the learning professions: A status report on teacher development in the United States and abroad.* National Staff Development Council.

Darling-Hammond, L., Hyler, M. E., & Gardner, M. (2017). *Effective teacher professional development.* Learning Policy Institute.

DeMonte, J. (2013). *High-quality professional development for teachers: Supporting teacher training to improve student learning.* Center for American Progress.

Desimone, L. M., & Garet, M. S. (2015). Best practices in teachers' professional development in the United States. *Psychology, Society, and Education, 3,* 252–263.

Fullan, M. (2003). *Change forces with a vengeance.* Routledge Falmer.

Fullan, M. (2006). *Turnaround leadership.* Jossey-Bass.

Fullan, M. (2007). *The new meaning of educational change* (4th ed.). Teachers College Press.

Fullan, M. (2008). *The six secrets of change.* Jossey-Bass.

Glanz, J. (2024). *Creating a culture of excellence: A School leader's guide to best practices in teaching, curriculum, professional development, supervision, and evaluation.* Rowman & Littlefield.

Gore, J. M., Miller, A., Fray, L., Harris, J., & Prieto, E. (2021). Improving student achievement through professional development: Results from a randomized controlled trial of Quality Teaching Rounds. *Teaching and Teacher Education, 101.* https://doi.org/10.1016/j.tate.2021.103297

Hadar, L. L., Ergas, O., Alpert, B., & Ariav, T. (2020). Rethinking teacher education in a VUCA world. *European Journal of Teacher Education,* 1–14. https://doi.org/10.1080/02619768.2020.1807513

Holmes, A. G. D. (2022). Researcher positionality - A consideration of its influence and place in qualitative research: A new researcher guide. *Shanlax International Journal of Education, 8*(4), 1–10.

House, R. J. (1976). A theory of charismatic leadership. In J. G. Hunt & L. L. Larson (Eds.), *Leadership: The cutting edge* (pp. 189–207). Southern Illinois University Press.

Hozer Mankal. (2006). *By-laws of the Israeli Ministry of Education.* https://www.proz.com/kudoz/hebrew-to-english/education-pedagogy/5257325-%D7%97%D7%95%D7%96%D7%A8-%D7%9E%D7%A0%D7%9B%22%D7%9C.html

Israeli Ministry of Education. (2020). *Transparency in education (Hebrew).* https://shkifut.education.gov.il/

Johnson, C. W., & Voelkel, R. H. (2019). Developing increased leader capacity to support effective PLC teams. *International Journal of Leadership in Education, 24*(3). https://doi.org/10.1080/13603124.2019.1600039

Korthagen, F., & Nuijten, E. (2022). *The power of reflection in teacher education and professional development.* Routledge.

Kraft, M. A., & Papay, J. P. (2014). Can professional environments in schools promote teacher development? Explaining heterogeneity in returns to teaching experience. *Educational Evaluation and Policy Analysis, 36*(4), 476–500.

Krasniqi, R. (2021). Principal's role in supporting teacher collaborative learning. *Research in Educational Administration and Leadership, 6*(4), 903–941.

Leithwood, K. A., & Jantzi, D. (2005). Transformational leadership. In B. Davies (Ed.), *The essentials of school leadership* (pp. 31–43). Corwin.

Lindstrom, P. H., & Speck, M. (2004). *The principal as professional development leader.* Corwin.

Macià, M., & García, I. (2016). Informal online communities and networks as a source of teacher professional development: A review. *Teaching and Teacher Education, 55*, 291–307.

Pan, H.-L. W., & Cheng, S.-H. (2023). Examining the impact of teacher learning communities on self-efficacy and professional learning: An application of the theory-driven evaluation. *Sustainability, 15*, 4771. https://doi.org/10.3390/su15064771

Popova, A., Evans, D. K., Breeding, M. E., & Arancibia, V. (2021). Teacher professional development around the world: The gap between evidence and practice. *The World Bank Research Observer, 37*(1), 107–136.

Postholm, M. B. (2012). Teachers' professional development: A theoretical review. *Educational Research, 54*(4), 405–429.

Rush, P. (2022). *The principal as a change agent.* https://www.learningcircle.co.nz/blog/the-principal-as-a-change-agent

Sancar, R., Atol, D., & Deryakula, D. (2021). A new framework for teachers' professional development. *Teaching and Teacher Education, 101.* https://doi.org/10.1016/j.tate.2021.103305

Sarason, S. (1982). *The culture of the school and the problem of change* (2nd ed.). Allyn & Bacon.

Starratt, R. J. (1995). *Leaders with vision: The quest for school renewal.* Corwin.

Sullivan, S., & Glanz, J. (2013). *Supervision that improves teaching: Strategies and techniques* (4th ed.). Corwin.

CHAPTER 4

NEEDED—COHERENT SYSTEM TRANSFORMATION TO BUILD CAPACITY AND LEVERAGE LEARNING DURING SYSTEM INNOVATION

Sally J. Zepeda
University of Georgia, USA

Grant M. Rivera
Marietta City Schools, USA

Beza Tefera Muzein
University of Georgia, USA

Kathryn Polley
University of Georgia, USA

ABSTRACT

In Chapter 4, Professor Zepeda and colleagues examine the lessons learned as a school district in the United States pressed forward to reform literacy instruction in grades 1 through 3 by moving to the Science of Reading. The complexities of transformational change on a district level are meticulously addressed. Coherence between the district and school levels underlying this system-wide change across eight schools is emphasized as critical to the change process. In addition, the attention to coherence in policies, practices, and processes illustrates that when school districts innovate, they can build capacity and leverage learning for adults. This chapter offers a unique contribution with insights into large-scale system transformation.

Keywords: Reform; school districts; educational policies; large-scale transformation; system wide change; coherence

---

Prefocus Guiding Questions

- *What professional and personal characteristics must successful transformational leaders possess?*
- *What actionable steps can leaders take to promote coherence during system transformation?*
- *How do leaders garner buy-in from teachers and staff when implementing large-scale system transformation?*

INTRODUCTION

This chapter examines the lessons learned as a school district in the United States pressed forward to transform literacy instruction in grades 1 through 3 by moving from a whole-language approach to the Science of Reading (SoR). The SoR is described as a scientifically and evidence-based approach that prioritizes direct, explicit, and systematic teaching of essential oral language skills such as phonics, phonemic awareness, vocabulary, fluency, and comprehension to transform literacy instruction (Shanahan, 2020; Snowling et al., 2022). The transformation was grounded in the belief that students had to have strong literacy skills as a foundation early in their academic careers to reduce opportunity gaps as they moved through later grades and into their postsecondary lives.

Leading a system transformation for the 2,650 students in grades K-3 across its eight elementary schools was not a single event but a comprehensive process. This transformation depended on coherence, a systematic approach to district leadership (Elmore et al., 2014; Honig, 2012; Moore Johnson et al., 2014). This approach incorporates shared language, interdepartmental collaboration, and a focus on creating success through aligned strategic goals. Coherence is crucial for building trust and unity as district leaders work to support school-level administrators and teachers. Moreover, the attention to coherence in policies, practices, and processes illustrated that when school districts innovate, they build capacity and leverage learning for the adults.

This chapter starts by reviewing the literature on transformational leadership and coherence. It then describes the district and provides a brief overview of the methods used to collect data across three years of engagement with the system. Next, it discusses the moving parts and their practical implications for juggling them.

LITERATURE REVIEW

Transformational Leadership

Educational research has consistently highlighted the important influence of leadership practices on teaching and learning outcomes (Bush, 2017; Leithwood & Jantzi, 1999). The transformational leadership theory gained substantial acceptance as a model that strongly emphasizes inspiration, vision, and the development of defined goals (Sun & Leithwood, 2012).

Transformational leaders simultaneously develop individuals while redesigning the organization and do so by creating environments and cultures that improve teaching and learning (Day et al., 2016). Transformational leaders inspire stakeholders to overcome barriers with compelling future visions (Bass & Riggio, 2006; Leithwood & Sun, 2012). To transform systems, efforts start at the district level to develop robust and equitable opportunities for learning by:

- Establishing a focus on learning—by persistently and publicly focusing their attention and that of others on learning and teaching (Knapp, 2003, p. 12).

This focus on learning includes intellectual stimulation through challenging assumptions, encouraging creativity, and providing information to improve staff practices (Khan et al., 2022; Sun & Leithwood, 2012). It also significantly contributes to employee job satisfaction (Puni et al., 2018). As important to transformation, system leaders stay connected to classroom practices and support instructional improvement.

- Building professional communities that value learning—by nurturing work cultures that value and support their members' learning (Knapp, 2003, p. 12).

Transformational leadership is contingent on the leader's ability to empower individuals to feel valued and motivated (Khan et al., 2022) while forging positive leader-member relationships (Elkins, 2003).

A major effort identified by Knapp (2003) and uplifted across the literature is coherence (Elmore et al., 2014; Fullan & Quinn, 2015). Without coherence, transformations risk not being implemented systematically or consistently.

Coherence

It is hardly likely that a system can transform in the absence of structures, processes, and procedures—all needed for coherence to "connect and align [the] work across the organization" (Elmore et al., 2014, p. 3). Coherence is the bedrock of transformation. Without it, district actions and decisions would become unpredictable, initiatives unsustainable, and fragmented leadership focus, leading to system overload and inefficiency. Transformative leaders create a vision and motivate others to achieve goals and objectives. Coherence ensures that transformative change is implemented systematically and consistently across the district (Fullan & Quinn, 2015). However, coherence goes deeper and "serves an interpersonal purpose–a way for people to make sense of their work and the work of others and its relationship to the system" (Zepeda et al., 2021, p. 25).

Coherence is the glue that connects "educator practices and organizational processes" (Elmore et al., 2014, p. 1). It supports the development of relationships built on a common understanding of ideas, the efforts needed to achieve goals, and mutual trust (Moore Johnson et al., 2014). It also provides stability during system innovation and transformation (Fullan & Quinn, 2015) and builds capacity (Cobb et al., 2018).

During transformation, the central office achieves coherence through purposeful efforts and the superintendent's decisive and visible leadership (Lanoue & Zepeda, 2018). Coherence is achieved, in part, when systems examine evidence from multiple sources. Examining evidence in the school community context also helps to differentiate support and bring clarity and collective understanding to lead in purposeful ways.

Coherence is also about building partnerships through mutual understanding between the central office and building levels. School leaders and teachers depend on productive, collaborative partnerships with the central office that "coherently focus on specific needs, provide the right resources, [and] attend to the professional learning needs of teachers and principals" (Zepeda et al., 2021, p. 136). Coherence can only be reached through the sustained efforts of leaders across every level of a school district.

CONTEXT OF THE DISTRICT

In the larger context, Schwartz (2024) reported that 38 states and the District of Columbia have either enacted laws or adopted new policies regarding evidence-based reading instruction since 2013. In 2024, the Georgia Early Literacy Act (House Bill 538) requires all teachers and leaders to be formally trained in structured literacy methods based on the SoR. The Marietta City School District is a small charter system in Georgia that serves approximately 8,700 PK-12 students across 13 schools and learning centers. Situated in the suburbs of a large city, Marietta City Schools (MCS) hosts a diverse student population, with approximately 68% of students qualifying for free or reduced lunch. MCS currently employs 916 certified staff to serve its PK-12 students.

During the 2021–2022 school year, MCS implemented a district-wide initiative to improve its students' literacy development. With the support of a multi-million-dollar grant, the district embarked on its initiative entitled *Literacy and Justice for All*, in which science of reading approaches would be implemented to promote the literacy growth of nearly the 2,650 students in grades K-3 across its 8 elementary schools. Literacy was more than just a set of skills—this effort was also about breaking life trajectories that can often lead to incarceration, unemployment, and mental health issues (Burk & Hasbrouck, 2023).

The SoR is a top priority in MCS, requiring teachers to transform their approaches to teaching reading and writing and for school principals to lead this work in their schools along with an instructional coach in every building and four SoR Facilitators whose time was divided across the eight elementary schools. The implementation of the SoR required the superintendent of MCS to strategize and lead through several moving parts.

METHODS

This research gathered qualitative data regarding system transformation over three academic years. Interviews and focus groups were conducted with central office leaders, principals, instructional coaches, SoR Facilitators, teachers, and Reading Specialists across the eight elementary schools within MCS. The principals and literacy instructional coaches of each school were interviewed two to three times each year. A wide range of topics was covered during these interviews, including participants' perspectives about professional learning, successes, and challenges in implementing the SoR, and relationship development within and across schools and the district central office. Not surprisingly, with any large-scale transformation, many moving parts illustrate the need for structures, procedures, and the deployment of key personnel to bring coherence of efforts.

MOVING PARTS

Transforming literacy instruction for nearly 2,650 K-3 students across 8 elementary schools—moving from a whole-language approach to the SoR—was not a linear process. Instead, this transformation involved complex, interconnected changes that created dynamic interplay, challenging and enriching the system's understanding of teaching and leading literacy. From the onset, several moving parts created the need to make interconnected changes in the structures and procedures and to add additional personnel to move forward with this work.

At the center of this work was the curriculum and instruction that had to change significantly while advancing through the initiation of the SoR. The new content and aligned pedagogical approaches necessitated changes in how teachers delivered literacy instruction, how leaders guided the work in their schools, how instructional coaches supported teachers, and how SoR Facilitators assisted the efforts across their assigned buildings. Structures and procedures needed to be developed or modified to elevate the transformation of literacy instruction across the district.

STRUCTURES AND PROCEDURES

The need to develop or refine various structures and procedures unfolded simultaneously, requiring decisive leadership tied to the system vision to manage each part while considering its relationship to other parts.

Moving Part 1: Development of the SoR Cycle

To lead the district through this major transition, a routinized system of SoR professional learning and assessment practices embedded in teachers' and leaders' work was needed. The system's developed SoR Cycle guides MCS's SoR professional learning, including the components detailed in Table 4.1.

A SoR Facilitator is assigned to a school to support these components by allocating time in the current configuration for four consecutive days and then two subsequent days across two weeks, constituting a "cycle."

The SoR Cycle promotes job-embedded learning aimed at: a) consistently communicating new information about the SoR to building-level leaders, instructional coaches, and teachers, b) supporting teaching and learning in the SoR in K-3 classrooms across the district, and c) providing professional learning on the application of pedagogical skills associated with SoR approaches to literacy instruction.

Moving Part 2: SoR Classroom Walkthrough Observations

A major part of the SoR Cycle is the SoR Classroom Walkthrough Observation. During each Cycle, the SoR Facilitator, the instructional coach,

TABLE 4.1 The Science of Reading (SoR) Cycle Format

DAYS 1–4	
Administrative overview	Takes place at the beginning of a SoR Cycle. The principal, assistant principal(s), instructional coach(es), and SoR Facilitator meet to review the SoR Cycle's implementation plan, SoR standards and elements to be used, review school logistics for the week, and preview the professional learning content for the knowledge professional learning community.
Learning walks	An informal walk that includes at least the instructional coach and SoR Facilitator to visit classrooms on the first day of the SoR Cycle to get a pulse on literacy instruction, assess professional learning, and offer support.
SoR classroom walkthrough observations [2.0]	Lasts 20-minutes using the SoR classroom walkthrough observation instrument. The coach uses the ratings to guide coaching conversations with teachers with the intent to improve practice. The ratings help to determine trends within the school and across schools to set short-term action plans related to professional learning.
Professional learning communities—knowledge session	Is (at minimum) a 45-minute grade level meeting in which the SoR Facilitator leads teachers through a professional learning session.
Professional learning communities—action session	Is a 45-minute grade level meeting in which the SoR Facilitator leads teachers through an action-based professional learning session connected to the previously held professional learning community knowledge session. A labsite is a professional learning model in which the SoR Facilitator, a teacher, or other school personnel leads instruction for other teachers to observe.
Implementation team	A vertical team with a minimum of one teacher per grade level. The intent of the implementation team is to dive deeper into the content of the SoR Cycle.
Administrative debrief	Takes place at the conclusion of a SoR Cycle. The principal, assistant principal(s), instructional coach (es), and SoR Facilitator meet to review the SoR Cycle's implementation plan, review SoR classroom walkthrough observation data, reflect on the SoR Cycle, review progress toward the previous SoR Cycle's goals, and generate short-term goals to be completed before next SoR Cycle begins.
Coaching the coach	Is protected time for the school's literacy instructional coach and the science of reading facilitator to collaborate. The time is differentiated and flexible to the needs of the instructional coach at the site. The SoR facilitator and instructional coach may use the time to delve deeper into content, research, review data, or brainstorm solutions to challenges.
DAYS 5–6	
Differentiated support days	Differentiated support days are built into the SoR Cycle to achieve short-term goals developed in the administrative Debrief. The support may include follow up planning or professional learning for groups or individuals, instructional modeling, co-teaching, co-planning, observation with immediate coaching conversation, data analysis, or other professional activities as appropriate.

building-level leaders, and other school personnel conduct up to 11 classroom walkthroughs that last a minimum of 20 minutes. The SoR Walkthrough was designed to a) ensure consistency of instructional practices, b) assess teachers' individual and holistic professional development needs, and c) drive coaching conversations to improve teachers' practice. During the third year of implementation, MCS codified the key literacy standards and associated elements, a series of SoR instructional strategies, and embedded these into a walkthrough instrument completed electronically (on a Google Form), enabling Walkthrough data to be housed instantly in a single location.

Through three years of innovating, efforts have a) simplified and streamlined the process, b) allowed for unified language regarding SoR practices, c) facilitated authentic and productive conversations about teachers' practices, and d) promoted reflection for teachers and others who are involved in the walkthrough process.

Moving Part 3: Changes in Professional Learning

The shift to the SoR brought major changes to teacher and leader professional learning. As a first major hurdle, the superintendent and literacy leaders set out to orient K-3 teachers and their building-level leaders to the emerging body of knowledge in the SoR. The system started professional learning approximately five months prior to the first year of implementation. Professional learning included all school leaders, instructional coaches, and teachers in grades 1 through 3.

The initial professional learning included post-planning sessions at the end of the spring and moved into a whole week in the summer. During the initial summer session, teams from each school were immersed in the SoR and spent considerable time developing implementation plans based on their school and system strategic plans.

Outside of the rigorous professional learning offered to teachers and staff during the SoR Cycles, nearly every school-wide professional development opportunity focused on literacy development. Each school's literacy instructional coach led professional learning in their school, sustaining the practices and supporting teachers' developing knowledge in between SoR Cycles.

To build capacity even further among the K-3 teachers, they were afforded opportunities to participate in advanced literacy training. This enabled teachers to earn certifications in the Orton-Gillingham approach and their state's endorsement in dyslexia instruction. Using grant funds, teachers who completed all of the required coursework for these advanced professional preparation sessions were issued a stipend for their time and effort.

PERSONNEL

Undeniably, teachers are the heart of teaching, and they engage daily in the complex work of teaching children. Teachers, school leaders, and instructional coaches have carried forward literacy instructional efforts.

Moving Part 4: SoR Facilitators

The SoR Facilitators coordinate the work embedded in the SoR Cycles. The SoR Facilitators are housed at the central office. However, they work intently and exclusively with two schools, supporting leaders and instructional coaches during the SoR Cycles and between them. During the first year of the SoR, the Facilitators were not employees of MCS; they were on loan from another system. The system needed SoR Facilitators who were available between SoR Cycles, had visibility, and could engage fully in the system as full-time employees. From the second year forward, the SoR Facilitators were full-time employees of MCS and increased from four in Year 3 working with grades K-3 to six, moving into Year 4 of this work expanding across K-8.

The SoR Facilitators provide regular professional development and help the system assess progress in implementing the SoR across all eight of its elementary schools. As MCS has continued to advance this transformation, the literacy needs at each school have evolved, creating the need to hire additional SoR Facilitators and modifying the job description to include overseeing the curriculum, literacy partnerships, assessments, and professional learning across the district.

Moving Part 5: Hiring Reading Specialists

Consistently assessing the literacy support needs of the K-3 teachers in MCS, in Year 3, the superintendent allocated funds to hire 41 Reading Specialists to provide intensive literacy support to students at each of the 8 districts' elementary schools. The position of the Reading Specialist was building-based, and allocations were determined based on the size and the literacy needs represented at each school. Allocations varied, with one school qualifying for eight Reading Specialists and another school qualifying for just one Reading Specialist. Principals were tasked with hiring the Reading Specialist in their buildings, with most principals opting to hire strong K-3 teachers to fill this new position.

Moving Part 6: Onboarding New Teachers

Given the demanding nature of professional learning in the SoR, onboarding new teachers proved challenging. Through a collaborative approach led by central office literacy leaders and the Instructional Coaches at each school site, new teachers participated in intensive professional learning sessions that brought them "up to speed" with the SoR concepts and pedagogical skills that had been introduced in previous years. The Instructional Coaches provided individualized support and feedback and planned lessons collaboratively.

New teachers were sometimes overwhelmed by the content delivered during intensive training sessions because they had to do "double time" learning by keeping up with new professional learning offered through the ongoing SoR Cycles. Along with navigating other "news" in their position (i.e., new curriculum, new school norms, new students, etc.), early-career teachers found that the amount of content and pedagogical skills that they were expected to retain and implement in their instruction was overwhelming, causing concerns of burnout among the new teachers.

PRACTICAL IMPLICATIONS FOR JUGGLING THE MOVING PARTS

Whether small or large-scale, transformation changes are often messy and fraught with multiple implementation dips as systems respond to steer the direction and speed of the work. There are no magic formulas that can be followed lock-step; however, there are structures that, if attended to, can lead to more coherent efforts that lead systems to the targeted mark.

People First, Always

The structures and procedures were complex and interconnected, necessitating the creation of a series of new structures and procedures, often at the same time. Systems are important, but people have to matter first. The most important work a leader does—regardless of title or position–is to work with system personnel in ways that prompt lifelong learning skills, inquiry, reflection, collaboration, and dedication to professional growth and development (Zepeda, 2017). However, there is more. Effective leaders ensure that their staff feel encouraged and supported in their professional growth. When teachers feel regarded as professionals, they are more likely to buy into school and district initiatives and that they are essential to this work (Moore Johnson et al., 2014).

The superintendent ensured teachers were adequately supported in their learning by creating structured time for district-level literacy leaders (i.e., SoR Facilitators) and school-based literacy instructional coaches to provide teachers with individualized support. As a result, teachers felt affirmed as professionals and motivated toward additional professional growth. This illustrates the importance of the leader's ability to make people feel individually cared for, motivated, and intellectually challenged (Khan et al., 2022).

Differentiated Structures for Professional Growth—Early-Career Teachers Need More

All school and system personnel need professional learning—and the structures to support growth must be differentiated. Influential leaders provide consistent and transparent structures for supporting the professional growth of teachers, especially those new to the profession (Moore Johnson, 2019). The district confronted challenges in catching early-career teachers "up to speed" on the content and pedagogical skills addressed in previous years.

Before the start of the school year, teachers new to the district completed a series of training modules in the SoR. They participated in the professional learning opportunities embedded in the SoR Cycles. As a system-wide practice, teachers met regularly with their literacy instructional coaches for individualized professional learning support beyond the SoR Cycle. With high expectations for professional learning, the superintendent ensured that new teachers felt supported in their professional growth, enabling them to see the value and promote buy-in to the district's vision for literacy.

Empower Others

Effective leaders trust their team's expertise (Day et al., 2016). Prior to the science of reading, principals had discretion regarding the literacy curriculum and resources used at each school. The transformation necessitated a uniform curriculum across all eight schools to align with the SoR and its foundation that prioritizes direct, explicit, and systematic teaching of essential oral language skills (e.g., phonics and phonemic awareness). Recognizing staff expertise, the superintendent formed a diverse task force of teachers, coaches, administrators, and literacy leaders to select a district-wide literacy curriculum.

Understanding that this new curricular shift would require supplemental professional learning support, the superintendent appointed a district-level literacy leader to take ownership of the new K-5 literacy curriculum.

As the district's resident expert on literacy, this leader offers additional support to teachers and building-based leaders, further bolstering buy-in to the districts' vision for literacy.

Assess Needs—The Work of Transformation Is Dynamic

Effective leaders consistently assess the need to advance the overall vision (Day et al., 2016), and they continuously scan the environment to adapt strategies and approaches to avoid detours that could threaten success. Advancing the SoR required a close examination of individual needs at each school. As the learning needs of the students became more evident, it became apparent that there was a need for additional literacy interventionalists at each school to offer intensive support to struggling students. As a result, funds were allocated to hire 41 full-time reading specialists to support K-3 classroom teachers in providing literacy instruction in a 10:1 student-teacher ratio.

Assessing the structures and embedded processes of professional learning in the SoR Cycles against the schools' needs made clear that the system needed to hire more SoR Facilitators so they could spend more time with fewer schools, providing even more comprehensive support to school personnel. Moreover, after gaining insight from the perspectives of the principals and instructional coaches, a decision was made that the SoR Facilitators would be hired as employees of the district rather than as consultants on loan from an external system.

Growing Pains and Momentary Disequilibrium

Transformation often results in growing pains, creating momentary disequilibrium. Modifications to systems were made to focus its efforts. These modifications sometimes created momentary disequilibrium as district personnel needed to develop policies and procedures almost seemingly "on the fly." To navigate the constantly changing nature of transformation, certain key qualities that promote ongoing growth and development are necessary (Bass, 1985; Carless et al., 2000). In practical application, a leader must use strategies congruent with the vision, foster staff growth, and promote innovative thinking.

The vision serves as the compass and helps to restore equilibrium during turbulence. In the case of leading the district through a significant shift in literacy instruction, the superintendent understood the importance of implementing a routine system for SoR professional learning and assessment to facilitate this transition. In collaboration with other leaders across the district, the SoR Cycle was developed and implemented to ensure coherence of what would occur in buildings and provide guidance to its leaders and instructional coaches as they transformed the teaching of literacy.

CONCLUSION

To fully embrace large-scale system transformation, those within the system must possess confidence in the direction of their leaders. Leaders bring coherence to the work of system transformation by creating synergy—promoting clarity and consistency as they juggle multiple moving parts. Changes to a system are sustained and embedded within the culture when leaders' decisions acknowledge the power of coherence, preventing the system from becoming a collection of seemingly random actions.

Superintendents can navigate and sustain systems by implementing processes to ensure that the policies, allocation of material resources, deployment of human resources, and the constellation of community voices move the system together. Coherence for school systems promotes a single, clear vision, minimizing distractions and maximizing the capacity needed to transform a system. For this district, transformation demanded all stakeholders' commitment to learn, apply, and refine structured literacy practices through consistent implementation, regular reflection, and data-driven adjustments.

CASE STUDY

Meadowview School District is a small, rural school system in the midwestern United States that serves approximately 10,000 students in 15 schools. The student population is racially diverse: nearly 50% of its students qualify for ESOL services, and about 30% receive special education services. Meadowview School District employs 900 certified teachers with an average of 8 years of teaching experience.

After noticing an influx in mental and emotional health challenges among the student population, the superintendent of Meadowview School District will propose a district-wide initiative to promote its students' social and emotional learning (SEL). This intensive SEL initiative, which will launch next school year, requires a major shift in teaching practices. Teachers in every discipline and grade level must integrate SEL concepts into their daily instruction. In addition, teachers will engage in weekly, job-embedded professional learning about SEL, requiring a significant commitment of time, effort, and emotional energy. Throughout the first year of the SEL initiative, students will be regularly surveyed to assess Meadowview School District's progress toward its new vision for student wellness.

Dr. Smith, the superintendent, has served in Meadowview School District for over 20 years. She hopes that her successful track record with boosting student achievement and retaining teachers will enable her to garner staff buy-in on this new SEL initiative. She is aware, however, that the success of this district-wide shift to SEL-integrated instruction relies heavily on the investment of building-level leaders and teachers.

During tomorrow's principals meeting, Dr. Smith will announce Meadowview School District's plans to launch this SEL initiative. In preparation for tomorrow's big announcement, Dr. Smith picks up her pen and begins drafting her major talking points.

REFLECTIONS ON THE CASE

- What might Dr. Smith consider before communicating her vision for Meadowview School District's SEL initiative?
- What steps could Dr. Smith take to garner buy-in from building-level leaders and teachers? How might Dr. Smith ensure staff feels adequately supported through this major instructional shift?
- Have you experienced a significant instructional shift as a teacher or leader? What challenges or successes did you encounter through this period of system transformation?

REFERENCES

Bass, B. (1985). *Leadership and performance beyond expectations*. Free Press.

Bass, B. M., & Riggio, R. E. (2006). *Transformational leadership*. Psychology Press.

Burk, K., & Hasbrouck, J. (2023). Connecting the science of reading to social justice: Introduction to the special section. *School Psychology, 38*(1), 4–6. https://doi.org/10.1037/spq0000536

Bush, T. (2017). The enduring power of transformational leadership. *Educational Management Administration & Leadership, 45*(4), 563–565. https://doi.org/10.1177/1741143217701827

Carless, S. A., Wearing, A. J., & Mann, L. (2000). A short measure of transformational leadership. *Journal of Business and Psychology, 14*(3), 389–405. https://doi.org/10.1023/A:1022991115523

Cobb, P., Jackson, K., Henrick, E., & Smith, T. M. (2018). *Systems for instructional improvement: Creating coherence from the classroom to the district office*. Harvard Education Press.

Day, C., Gu, Q., & Sammons, P. (2016). The impact of leadership on student outcomes: How successful school leaders use transformational and instructional strategies to make a difference. *Educational Administration Quarterly, 52*(2), 221–258. https://doi.org/10.1177/0013161X15616863

Elkins, S. L. (2003). Transformational learning in leadership and management positions. *Human Research Development Quarterly, 14*(3), 239–363. https://doi.org/10.1002/hrdq.1071

Elmore, R. F., Foreman, M. L., Stosich, E. L., & Bocala, C. (2014). *The internal coherence assessment protocol & developmental framework: Building organizational capacity for instructional improvement in schools.* Strategic Education Research Partnership Institute.

Fullan, M., & Quinn, J. (2015). *Coherence: The right drivers in action for schools, districts, and systems.* Corwin Press.

Georgia Early Literacy Act, H.B. 538, 118th Cong. (2024). https://www.billtrack50.com/billdetail/1583404

Honig, M. I. (2012). District central office leadership as teaching: How central office administrators support principals' development as instructional leaders. *Educational Administration Quarterly, 48*(4), 733–774. https://doi.org/10.1177/0013161X12443258

Khan, I. U., Amin, R. U., & Saif, N. (2022). Individualized consideration and idealized influence of transformational leadership: Mediating role of inspirational motivation and intellectual stimulation. *International Journal of Leadership in Education,* 1–11. https://doi.org/10.1080/13603124.2022.2076286

Knapp, M. S. (2003). Professional development as a policy pathway. *Review of Research in Education, 27*(1), 109-157. http://www.jstor.org/stable/3568129?origin=JSTOR-pdf

Lanoue, P. D., & Zepeda, S. J. (2018). *The emerging work of today's superintendent: Leading schools and communities to educate all children.* Rowman & Littlefield. [Jointly published by the American School Superintendents Association].

Leithwood, K., & Jantzi, D. (1999). Transformational school leadership effects: A replication. *School Effectiveness and School Improvement, 10*(4), 451–479. https://doi.org/10.1076/SESI.10.4.451.3495

Leithwood, K., & Sun, J. (2012). The nature and effects of transformational school leadership: A meta-analytic review of unpublished research. *Educational Administration Quarterly, 48*(3), 387–423. https://doi.org/10.1177/0013161X11436268

Moore Johnson, S. (2019). *Where teachers thrive: Organizing schools for success.* Harvard Education Press.

Moore Johnson, S., Marietta, G., Higgins, M. C., Mapp, K. L., & Grossman, A. S. (2014). *Achieving coherence in district improvement: Managing the relationship between the central office and schools.* Harvard Education Press.

Puni, A., Mohammed, I., & Asamoah, E. (2018). Transformational leadership and job satisfaction: The moderating effect of contingent reward. *Leadership & Organization Development Journal, 39*(4), 522–537. https://doi.org/10.1108/LODJ-11-2017-0358

Schwartz, S. (2024, May 2). Which states have passed "science of reading" laws? What's in them? *Education Week.* https://www.edweek.org/teaching-learning/which-states-have-passed-science-of-reading-laws-whats-in-them/2022/07.

Shanahan, T. (2020). What constitutes a science of reading instruction? *Reading Research Quarterly, 55*(S1), 235–247. https://doi.org/10.1002/rrq.349

Snowling, M. J., Hulme, C., & Nation, K. (Eds.). (2022). *The science of reading: A handbook* (2nd ed.). Wiley Blackwell. https://doi.org/10.1002/9781119705116

Sun, J., & Leithwood, K. (2012). Transformational school leadership effects on student achievement. *Leadership and Policy in Schools, 11*(4), 418–451. https://doi.org/10.1080/15700763.2012.681001

Zepeda, S. J. (2017). *Instructional supervision: Applying tools and concepts.* Routledge.

Zepeda, S. J., Derrington, M. L., & Lanoue, P. D. (2021). *Developing the organizational culture of the central office: Collaboration, connectivity, and coherence.* Routledge.

ADDITIONAL READINGS

Gewertz, C. (2021, May 4). States to schools: Teach reading the right way. *Education Week.* https://www.edweek.org/teaching-learning/states-to-schools-teach-reading-the-right-way/2020/02.

Leithwood, K., Harris, A., & Hopkins, D. (2020). Seven strong claims about successful school leadership revisited. *School Leadership & Management, 40*(1), 5–22. https://doi.org/10.1080/13632434.2019.1596077

CHAPTER 5

LEADING CHANGE THROUGH INSTRUCTIONAL LEADERSHIP

Haim Shaked
Hemdat College of Education, Israel

ABSTRACT

In Chapter 5, Professor Shaked explores the conceptual framework of instructional leadership within the broader context of transformational school leadership, highlighting its critical role in facilitating change in schools. Not too long ago, instructional leadership was not viewed as a principal's primary or at least a very important responsibility. More and more school systems now, though not enough, have paid closer attention to the importance of instructional leadership. Instructional leaders primarily aim to transform teaching and learning in alignment with the school's mission, evaluate instruction and programs, and facilitate curriculum and professional development by creating professional learning communities to promote student learning and achievement. The chapter focuses on the four main elements of instructional leadership: instructional vision, instructional program, instructional climate, and teacher development. Each element is addressed in detail, drawing from extant literature and research and drawing practical implications.

Keywords: Principals; facilitating change; instructional change; learning communities; school mission; teacher development

> *Prefocus Guiding Questions*
>
> - What is instructional leadership, and why is it foundational for transformative change in schools?
> - What are the core elements of instructional leadership, and how do each contribute to improving educational outcomes?
> - Can you identify examples from your own experience or observed practices where core elements of instructional leadership were successfully implemented? What were the results?

INTRODUCTION

This chapter underscores the pivotal role of instructional leadership in driving educational transformation within schools, presenting a thorough analysis of how instructional leadership forms the foundation for school change. Initially, the chapter defines instructional leadership and delineates its fundamental aspects. It then identifies the four core elements of instructional leadership: instructional vision, instructional program, instructional climate, and teacher development. It then explores how these four core elements can facilitate school change by applying transformational leadership principles. This chapter highlights the direct impact of the four core elements of instructional leadership on educational outcomes and demonstrates how they contribute to a dynamic and progressive educational environment.

LITERATURE REVIEW

What Is Instructional Leadership

Instructional leadership is nearing its 100th anniversary, having been a topic of scholarly research since 1926 (Gray, 1934). This approach remains a central theme in educational leadership (Hallinger et al., 2020). School principals are still recognized as pivotal instructional leaders, critical for enhancing student academic outcomes (Cox & Mullen, 2023; Hou et al., 2019). As such, principals are tasked with prioritizing effective teaching and learning implementations within their schools (Shaked, 2023). This involves their active involvement in various activities designed to improve the curriculum and endorse teaching strategies that foster effective student learning (Bellibaş et al., 2022; Liu et al., 2021).

As instructional leaders, principals significantly influence student achievement through indirect avenues. Their impact is mediated by factors like instructional programs, school culture, and, notably, the teaching strategies used by educators (Murphy et al., 2016). Instructional leadership focuses on optimizing instructional time for high-quality teaching and promoting ongoing professional development for teachers (Hallinger et al., 2020). This leadership style is built on the proven relationship between the quality of instruction and student performance. Studies confirm that teaching quality is the most significant school-based factor affecting student results (Burroughs et al., 2019; Gershenson, 2016), outweighing other factors such as curricular programs or student grouping strategies. Achieving high-quality instruction, essential for student success, requires continuous support and guidance from principals as instructional leaders (Goldring et al., 2015).

The research underscores that school leadership is only second to classroom teaching in its impact on student learning (Leithwood et al., 2020). There is a well-established link between instructional leadership and improved educational outcomes, such as better teaching quality and elevated student achievement (Hou et al., 2019; Mitchell et al., 2015). This connection holds across different educational levels—from elementary to high schools—and in various institutions, including public, private, and charter schools. The benefits of instructional leadership are also apparent in diverse settings, ranging from urban to suburban environments (Cox & Mullen, 2023; Shatzer et al., 2014).

The strong empirical evidence linking principals' direct involvement in instructional activities to quality teaching and student success has prompted scholars to champion instructional leadership as a critical priority in contemporary education (Hallinger et al., 2020). Consequently, academic researchers and educational practitioners concur that today's school principals should emphasize instructional leadership as a central element of their responsibilities. Modern principals are increasingly expected, sometimes even mandated, to lead in this area, concentrating on teaching and learning and deeply engaging with curricular and instructional issues (Bellibaş et al., 2022; Liu et al., 2021). As instructional leaders, principals are entrusted with creating an environment that supports classroom instruction, ultimately fostering better student learning and improved academic outcomes (Glickman et al., 2024).

The Four Core Elements of Instructional Leadership

Over time, various frameworks have been developed to elucidate the concept of instructional leadership. One of the most prominent frameworks, introduced by Hallinger and Murphy (1985) almost 40 years ago, remains widely referenced in the field of instructional leadership research (Hallinger et al., 2020; Hallinger & Wang, 2015). This framework outlines three key dimensions, each encompassing several specific functions, totaling ten in all. The first dimension focuses on defining the school's mission through two functions: (1) Establishing the school's instructional objectives and (2) Communicating these objectives to all relevant stakeholders. The second dimension, managing the instructional program, involves three functions: (3) Coordinating the curriculum, (4) Supervising and evaluating teaching, and (5) Monitoring student progress. The third dimension, fostering a positive school learning environment, includes five functions: (6) Safeguarding instructional time; (7) Offering incentives for teacher motivation; (8) Encouraging student learning; (9) Supporting ongoing professional development for staff; and (10) Ensuring frequent, high-quality interactions with teachers and students.

Building on similar concepts, Weber (1989) proposed another framework for instructional leadership, which identifies five critical aspects: (1) Defining the school's mission; (2) Managing curriculum and instruction; (3) Supervising teaching; (4) Monitoring student progress; and (5) Evaluating the instructional environment.

The third framework, presented by Blase and Blase (2000), delineates two central themes and 11 strategies of instructional leadership that significantly impact teacher practices. The first theme, "talking with teachers to promote reflection," includes five strategies: (1) Offering suggestions, (2) Providing feedback, (3) Modeling, (4) Engaging in inquiry while soliciting advice and opinions, and (5) Extending praise. The second theme, "encouraging professional growth," consists of six strategies: (1) Focusing on the study of teaching and learning; (2) Promoting collaboration among educators; (3) Building coaching relationships; (4) Supporting the redesign of programs; (5) Integrating adult learning principles into staff development; and (6) Applying action research for instructional decision-making.

A fourth framework by Stronge and colleagues (2008), derived from an extensive literature review, outlines five essential characteristics of instructional leadership that principals use to meet instructional objectives. These characteristics include (1) Establishing and maintaining a clear vision for the school that defines learning goals and mobilizes community support to achieve them; (2) Distributing leadership roles to amplify teacher expertise and leadership; (3) Leading a community of professional learners and facilitating significant staff development opportunities; (4) Applying evidence and factual information to guide instructional decisions; and (5) Monitoring instructional practices to ensure effective implementation of curricula and teaching techniques.

Given the fundamental alignment across various instructional leadership frameworks, synthesizing them could prove beneficial. A detailed and comprehensive examination of these frameworks to pinpoint their shared components could lead to creating an integrated model. From such an integration, four core elements central to instructional leadership emerge: (1) Instructional vision: Developing and garnering support for a school vision focused on student learning and achievement objectives. (2) Instructional program: Coordinating, supervising, guiding, and monitoring the teaching and learning processes within the school to ensure effective instructional practices and outcomes. (3) Instructional climate: Establishing a positive and achievement-oriented academic atmosphere to enhance the teaching and learning environment is vital. (4) Teacher development: Fostering the continuous professional development of teachers, ensuring they consistently improve their instructional methods throughout their careers (Shaked, 2023). Table 5.1 demonstrates how the dimensions, functions, and characteristics of instructional leadership, as detailed in existing frameworks, correspond with these four core elements of instructional leadership.

The First Element: How Instructional Vision Supports School Change

Effective school leaders are adept at articulating, promoting, and rallying support for a shared vision that centers on student learning and achievement. This process begins with the leader's ability to clearly define and communicate the educational goals and the paths to achieving them (Munter & Correnti, 2017). By involving faculty, staff, and other stakeholders in formulating this vision, leaders ensure that it resonates on a broad scale and reflects the collective aspirations and values of the school community (Willis et al., 2024). Once established, the vision serves as a rallying point, continually referenced and reinforced through school activities, meetings, and professional development. Leaders maintain momentum by celebrating milestones and exemplifying the vision through their daily actions and decisions, thus embedding these ideals into the school's culture (Woods & Wilhelm, 2020).

Developing a coherent instructional vision that aligns with transformational leadership principles involves several strategic steps. Leaders must first ensure that the vision highlights academic goals and integrates the broader aims of inspiring and motivating staff toward these common objectives. This requires leaders to be visionary yet approachable, encouraging open dialogue that invites diverse perspectives and fosters a sense of ownership among all staff members (Asbari et al., 2020). Workshops and collaborative sessions can be effective in this context, as they allow stakeholders to contribute actively to shaping the vision. Moreover, successful leaders employ clear, consistent communication and provide the necessary resources to support the vision's implementation. By aligning the school's policies, procedures, and professional development efforts with the articulated vision, leaders facilitate a cohesive and focused approach to school transformation (O'Reilly & Chatman, 2020).

The significance of a clear instructional vision cannot be overstated in its role in setting the direction for school change and ensuring sustained commitment to educational excellence. A well-defined and compelling vision provides a framework for decision-making and strategic planning, guiding the school through challenges and opportunities. It helps prioritize

TABLE 5.1 The Four Core Elements of Instructional Leadership Deriving From Prevalent Frameworks of Instructional Leadership (Shaked, 2023)

Key Element	Frameworks' Dimensions/Functions/Themes/Strategies				
	Hallinger and Murphy (1985)		Weber (1989)	Blase and Blase (2000)	Stronge et al. (2008)
Instructional vision	Framing school goals		Defining the school mission		Building and sustaining a school vision
	Communicating school goals				
Instructional program	Coordinating the curriculum		Managing curriculum and instruction		Monitoring curriculum and instruction
	Supervising and evaluating instruction		Supervising teaching	Talking with teachers to promote reflection	Using data to make instructional decisions
				Making suggestions	
				Giving feedback	
				Modeling	
				Using inquiry and soliciting advice and opinions	
	Monitoring student progress		Monitoring student progress		

80 • Haim Shaked

Instructional climate	Developing a positive school learning climate	Protecting instructional time		Assessing the instructional climate		
			Providing incentives for teachers		Giving praise	
			Providing incentives for learning			
			Maintaining high visibility			
Teacher development		Promoting professional development		Promoting professional growth		Leading a learning community
					Emphasizing the study of teaching and learning	
					Supporting collaboration efforts	
					Developing coaching relationships	
					Encouraging the redesign of programs	
					Applying the principles of adult learning, growth, and development	
					Implementing action research	
						Sharing leadership

initiatives that directly contribute to the vision, thereby maximizing the impact of resources and efforts. Furthermore, a clear vision fosters an environment of stability and predictability, which is crucial during periods of change. It keeps the entire school community aligned toward long-term goals, even as they navigate the complexities of daily operations and external pressures. Ultimately, a strong instructional vision acts as a north star, keeping the school focused on its mission of enhancing student outcomes and maintaining a steadfast commitment to improvement and excellence.

The Second Element: How Instructional Program Supports School Change

Instructional leadership is pivotal in coordinating, guiding, and monitoring teaching and learning processes within a school. As instructional leaders, school principals are tasked with ensuring that the curriculum delivered is relevant, rigorous, and aligned with educational standards and objectives (Ma & Marion, 2021). This involves selecting and promoting effective instructional strategies that cater to diverse learner needs and assessing these methods' efficacy in achieving desired educational outcomes (Murphy et al., 2016). Effective leaders frequently engage in classroom observations and provide constructive feedback, fostering an environment where continuous improvement is encouraged and facilitated. By keeping a close watch on the delivery and quality of instruction, they help maintain a standard of excellence and adaptability in teaching practices (Hallinger et al., 2020).

Developing a well-structured instructional program requires leaders to embody transformational leadership, inspiring and motivating staff toward a shared vision for student achievement (Anderson, 2017). This begins with clear communication of the educational goals and the strategies to achieve them, ensuring that all team members understand and are committed to their roles in this collective journey. Leaders can foster a sense of ownership and enthusiasm by involving teachers in the decision-making process, particularly in areas that affect their classroom practices. Regular professional development workshops and collaborative planning sessions are vital, as they help align individual teaching methods with the overall educational objectives and encourage the sharing of innovative practices. Furthermore, by setting high expectations and demonstrating confidence in their staff's abilities, leaders can inspire teachers to strive for higher levels of performance and engagement (Bakker et al., 2023).

Systematic improvements in the instructional program serve as a catalyst for broader school changes by setting a precedent for excellence and innovation. When instructional leaders focus on enhancing the curriculum and pedagogy, these changes can permeate various aspects of the school culture, influencing everything from student engagement to staff morale. Over time, the continuous refinement of teaching methods and curricular offerings can significantly improve student learning outcomes, elevating the school's overall performance. When communicated effectively to the wider school community, such progress can enhance the school's reputation, attract better resources, and instill a culture of pride and achievement. A robust instructional program supports and actively drives school change, leading to a more dynamic and effective educational environment.

The Third Element: How Instructional Climate Supports School Change

Creating a positive instructional climate conducive to academic achievement is a central task for instructional leaders to foster an environment that prioritizes and supports student learning (Dutta & Sahney, 2022). Such leaders focus on setting high expectations for both students and teachers, establishing a school-wide ethos that values hard work, commitment, and the pursuit of excellence. Strategies to cultivate this environment include clear communication of goals and expectations and consistent enforcement of policies that promote academic rigor (Jalapang & Raman, 2020). Additionally, fostering a culture of trust and respect among staff and students is crucial, as it encourages open dialogue and collaboration, necessary for effective teaching and learning. Leaders also emphasize the importance of a supportive environment by providing resources and interventions that address the varied needs of students, thus ensuring that each student has the opportunity to succeed (Walter et al., 2021).

To develop a positive instructional climate, instructional leaders draw upon principles of inspiring and motivating staff and students toward a shared goal. This process involves articulating a clear and compelling vision for the school and engaging all members of the school community in the vision's realization (Bakker et al., 2023). Leaders use recognition and rewards to motivate and sustain engagement, highlighting achievements and best practices that align with the school's objectives. Regular meetings and professional development sessions are leveraged to reinforce the school's values and strategies, encouraging continuous improvement and innovation. Moreover, by modeling their values, leaders build credibility and influence, inspiring others to adopt similar attitudes and behaviors that contribute to a positive instructional climate (Asbari et al., 2020).

The instructional ambiance within a school is a powerful lever for broader school change, significantly influencing student outcomes and overall school performance. A positive instructional climate encourages students to engage more deeply with their learning, promotes higher levels of attendance and participation, and reduces behavioral issues. A supportive and collaborative environment enhances job satisfaction and professional growth for teachers, increasing teaching efficacy. Over time, these improvements in the learning environment and teaching quality contribute to higher student achievement and school performance. Thus, by developing a positive instructional climate, leaders can initiate a continuous improvement cycle that benefits individual students and teachers and elevates the entire school community.

The Fourth Element: How Teacher Development Supports School Change

Instructional leaders play a critical role in fostering continuous professional growth for teachers, recognizing that developing teaching skills is essential for enhancing classroom instruction and driving school-wide change (Svendsen, 2020). Leaders invest in professional development programs tailored to their staff's diverse needs and career stages to support and encourage teacher learning. This includes workshops and training sessions introducing new teaching techniques and subject-specific content (Sancar et al., 2021). Mentoring programs pair less experienced teachers with seasoned veterans to provide guidance, support, and knowledge sharing. Leaders also promote forming collaborative learning communities within the school, where teachers can regularly meet to discuss challenges, share best practices, and collaboratively solve problems. These communities help to sustain a culture of learning and adaptability among staff, which is crucial for effective teaching and personal growth (Bellibaş et al., 2022).

To develop continuous professional growth for teachers, instructional leaders articulate a clear vision for professional development that aligns with the school's broader objectives, encouraging teachers to see their personal growth as integral to the school's success (Bakker et al., 2023). Leaders foster a supportive atmosphere that values ongoing learning and innovation, making it clear that professional development is a priority. They provide time and resources for teachers to engage in learning activities, and they recognize and celebrate professional achievements as part of the school's culture. By doing so, leaders not only motivate teachers to engage in professional growth activities but also help them understand how these activities contribute to the overarching goals of the school (Anderson, 2017; O'Reilly & Chatman, 2020).

Investing in faculty's continuous professional development serves to refine and improve instructional practices and acts as a catalyst for broader school change. When teachers are equipped with the latest educational strategies and continually improve their skills, the quality of instruction across the school is enhanced, leading to improved student outcomes. Moreover, a commitment to professional growth helps to attract and retain high-quality teaching staff, contributing to a stable and motivated faculty. This ongoing investment in teacher development creates a dynamic and responsive learning environment where students and teachers are engaged and motivated to achieve at high levels. Over time, this focus on professional growth fosters a culture of excellence and innovation in the school, driving significant changes in how the school operates and is perceived within the community.

CONCLUSION

This chapter aimed to provide current and aspiring school leaders with the knowledge and tools to lead educational change effectively. It emphasized the crucial role of instructional leadership in spearheading educational transformation within schools and offered a detailed analysis of how instructional leadership underpins school reform. By examining the four core elements of instructional leadership—instructional vision, instructional program, instructional climate, and teacher development—the chapter suggested a nuanced exploration of how these elements facilitate significant change through applying transformational leadership principles. Equipping leaders with the strategic insight necessary to implement practices that yield sustainable improvements, this chapter sought to prepare school leaders to understand and actively shape the educational landscape, ensuring that their schools are responsive and adaptable in the face of evolving educational challenges.

CASE STUDY

Rivers School, a middle school in a major Israeli city, serves a diverse student body of 450 in grades 7–9. With a teaching staff of 45, the school has traditionally emphasized a broad educational experience. Recently, however, it has encountered challenges with student engagement and the relevancy of its teaching methods. Principal Ruth Miller, leading the school for five years, is committed to a comprehensive overhaul of the school's instructional program.

Motivated by the latest findings in educational effectiveness, Principal Miller launched a school-wide reform aimed at modernizing the instructional approach. Her vision was to adopt teaching methods incorporating more collaborative activities and technology use, setting a new standard for excellence and innovation at Rivers School.

To implement this vision, she organized strategic planning sessions with her staff to co-develop a new curriculum framework. This framework focuses on critical thinking, creativity, and technology integration in daily lessons tailored to meet the diverse needs of Rivers School's students. This includes the use of multilingual resources and culturally responsive teaching methods.

Despite these efforts, the transformation faced significant hurdles. A clear lack of a consistently communicated instructional vision led to confusion and uneven commitment within the school community. Without a cohesive understanding of the new instructional strategies' objectives and advantages, teachers and parents were left skeptical of the changes.

In addition, while Principal Miller expected teachers to adopt these new methodologies, there was a noticeable deficiency in support for teacher development. The necessary professional development programs to equip teachers with the skills and confidence to implement these strategies were lacking. As a result, teachers were expected to improve without sufficient training or resources.

REFLECTIONS ON THE CASE

- How could Principal Miller have more effectively communicated her instructional vision to ensure school-wide alignment and support?
- What steps should be taken to provide meaningful and effective professional development that aligns with the new instructional strategies at Rivers School?
- Considering the initial setbacks, what can be done to revitalize the reform efforts and sustain long-term improvements in teaching and learning at the school?

REFERENCES

Anderson, M. (2017). Transformational leadership in education: A review of existing literature. *International Social Science Review, 93*(1), 1–13.

Asbari, M., Santoso, P. B., & Prasetya, A. B. (2020). Elitical and antidemocratic transformational leadership critics: Is it still relevant? *International Journal of Social, Policy, and Law, 1*(1), 12–16.

Bakker, A. B., Hetland, J., Olsen, O. K., & Espevik, R. (2023). Daily transformational leadership: A source of inspiration for follower performance? *European Management Journal, 41*(5), 700–708.

Bellibaş, M. Ş., Polatcan, M., & Kılınç, A. Ç. (2022). Linking instructional leadership to teacher practices: The mediating effect of shared practice and agency in learning effectiveness. *Educational Management Administration & Leadership, 50*(5), 812–831.

Blase, J., & Blase, J. (2000). Effective instructional leadership: Teachers' perspectives on how principals promote teaching and learning in schools. *Journal of Educational Administration, 38*(2), 130–141.

Burroughs, N., Gardner, J., Lee, Y., Guo, S., Touitou, I., Jansen, K., & Schmidt, W. (2019). *Teaching for excellence and equity: Analyzing teacher characteristics, behaviors and student outcomes with TIMSS.* Springer.

Cox, J. S., & Mullen, C. A. (2023). Impacting student achievement: Principals' instructional leadership practice in two Title I rural schools. *Journal of School Leadership, 33*(1), 3–25.

Dutta, V., & Sahney, S. (2022). Relation of principal instructional leadership, school climate, teacher job performance and student achievement. *Journal of Educational Administration, 60*(2), 148–166.

Gershenson, S. (2016). Linking teacher quality, student attendance, and student achievement. *Education Finance and Policy, 11*(2), 125–149.

Glickman, C. D., Gordon, S. P., Ross-Gordon, J. M., & Solis, R. (2024). *Supervision and instructional leadership: A developmental approach* (11th ed.). Pearson.

Goldring, E., Grissom, J. A., Neumerski, C. M., Murphy, J., Blissett, R., & Porter, A. (2015). *Making time for instructional leadership.* Wallace Foundation.

Gray, W. S. (1934). Evidence of the need of capable instructional leadership. *The Elementary School Journal, 34*(6), 417–426.
Hallinger, P., Gümüş, S., & Bellibaş, M. Ş. (2020). Are principals instructional leaders yet? A science map of the knowledge base on instructional leadership, 1940-2018. *Scientometrics, 122*(3), 1629–1650.
Hallinger, P., & Murphy, J. (1985). Assessing the instructional management behavior of principals. *The Elementary School Journal, 86*(2), 217–247.
Hallinger, P., & Wang, W. C. (2015). *Assessing instructional leadership with the principal instructional management rating scale.* Springer.
Hou, Y., Cui, Y., & Zhang, D. (2019). Impact of instructional leadership on high school student academic achievement in China. *Asia Pacific Education Review, 20*(4), 543–558.
Jalapang, I., & Raman, A. (2020). Effect of instructional leadership, principal efficacy, teacher efficacy and school climate on students' academic achievements. *Academic Journal of Interdisciplinary Studies, 9*(3), 82–92.
Leithwood, K., Harris, A., & Hopkins, D. (2020). Seven strong claims about successful school leadership revisited. *School Leadership & Management, 40*(1), 5–22.
Liu, Y., Bellibaş, M. Ş., & Gümüş, S. (2021). The effect of instructional leadership and distributed leadership on teacher self-efficacy and job satisfaction: Mediating roles of supportive school culture and teacher collaboration. *Educational Management Administration & Leadership, 49*(3), 430–453.
Ma, X., & Marion, R. (2021). Exploring how instructional leadership affects teacher efficacy: A multilevel analysis. *Educational Management Administration & Leadership, 49*(1), 188–207.
Mitchell, R. M., Kensler, L. A., & Tschannen-Moran, M. (2015). Examining the effects of instructional leadership on school academic press and student achievement. *Journal of School Leadership, 25*(2), 223–251.
Munter, C., & Correnti, R. (2017). Examining relations between mathematics teachers' instructional vision and knowledge and change in practice. *American Journal of Education, 123*(2), 171–202.
Murphy, J., Neumerski, C. M., Goldring, E., Grissom, J., & Porter, A. (2016). Bottling fog? The quest for instructional management. *Cambridge Journal of Education, 46*(4), 455–471.
O'Reilly, C. A., & Chatman, J. A. (2020). Transformational leader or narcissist: How grandiose narcissists can create and destroy organizations and institutions? *California Management Review, 62*(3), 5–27.
Sancar, R., Atal, D., & Deryakulu, D. (2021). A new framework for teachers' professional development. *Teaching and Teacher Education, 101*, 103305.
Shaked, H. (2023). *New explorations for instructional leaders: How principals can promote teaching and learning effectively.* Rowman & Littlefield.
Shatzer, R. H., Caldarella, P., Hallam, P. R., & Brown, B. L. (2014). Comparing the effects of instructional and transformational leadership on student achievement: Implications for practice. *Educational Management Administration & Leadership, 42*(4), 445–459.
Stronge, J. H., Richard, H. B., & Catano, N. (2008). *Qualities of effective principals.* Association for Supervision and Curriculum Development.

Svendsen, B. (2020). Inquiries into teacher professional development—what matters? *Education, 140*(3), 111–130.
Walter, E. M., Beach, A. L., Henderson, C., Williams, C. T., & Ceballos-Madrigal, I. (2021). Understanding conditions for teaching innovation in postsecondary education: Development and validation of the Survey of Climate for Instructional Improvement (SCII). *International Journal of Technology in Education, 4*(2), 166–199.
Weber, J. (1989). Leading the instructional program. In S. C. Smith & P. K. Piele (Eds.), *School leadership: Handbook for excellence* (2nd ed., pp. 191–224). ERIC Clearinghouse on Educational Management.
Willis, C., LaVenia, K. N., & Lasater, K. (2024). Compassionate leadership through instructional vision for special education. In K. Lasater & K. N. LaVenia (Eds.), *Compassionate leadership for school improvement and renewal* (pp. 191–211). Information Age Publishing.
Woods, D. M., & Wilhelm, A. G. (2020). Learning to launch complex tasks: How instructional visions influence the exploration of the practice. *Mathematics Teacher Educator, 8*(3), 105–119.

CHAPTER 6

TRANSFORMING TEACHING QUALITY WITH INTELLIGENT ACCOUNTABILITY

Helen M. Hazi
West Virginia University, USA

ABSTRACT

In Chapter 6, Professor Hazi tackles several taken-for-granted notions about teacher evaluation, which she decries as a failure. Instead, she introduces the concept of "intelligent accountability," which represents a system that can transform teaching and learning, encourage participatory leadership, and promote a professional learning community, all aspects of transformational leadership. She presents this concept as a way to think about helping teachers transform and account for their practice through self-reflection and evaluation. The role of team teaching, peer observation, self-evaluation, and evidence literacy are explored within a system of intelligent accountability and as a way for principals to transform and improve individuals and groups of teachers. She highlights a school known as Corbett Prep, an independent day school where teachers team to plan, teach, and assess instruction. Her work provides guidance to educational leaders who are dissatisfied with traditional practices of teacher evaluation with promising practices for change.

Keywords: Teacher evaluation; reform; self-evaluation; team teaching; teaching observation; educational change

> **Prefocus Guiding Questions**
>
> - *How is your school held accountable (federal/state/local) for student performance and teacher quality?*
> - *What are the consequences, both benefits and challenges, of an accountability system?*
> - *What would improve the accountability system?*

INTRODUCTION

In a post-COVID world, principals in the US are challenged with student learning loss, absences, and discipline; school shootings and book bans; and teacher shortages and low morale amidst demands for increased achievement. In addition, accountability in education has taken many forms including new standards, legislation, and regulation with sanctions, memoranda and guidance, targeted funding, ever-increasing surveillance at the state and federal levels, and school takeovers. While it intends to increase teacher and school quality, educational accountability becomes dysfunctional when it narrowly focuses on proxies such as student test scores. "[B]eneath this admirable rhetoric, the real focus is on performance indicators chosen for ease of measure and control rather than because they measure quality of performance accurately" (O'Neill, 2002, p. 54). Many existing accountability schemes undermine professional judgment, result in more detailed centralized control, and promote "a culture of suspicion, low morale, and may ultimately lead to professional cynicism" (p. 57).

However, accountability is neither good nor bad, but a necessary function of institutions to account to its stakeholders how it has expended taxpayer funds on its mission. It is how accountability becomes construed and used that makes it dysfunctional, "malpractice," and "educational vandalism" (O'Neill, 2013). When it was adapted from business into education, teachers may have lost sight of their responsibility, which includes accounting for student learning (Noddings, 2007). Only recently has accountability been made more specific, linked to student achievement, and tied to teachers' job performance.

O'Neill (2002, p. 58) calls educators to engage in *intelligent accountability*: to "give an account of what they have done and of their successes or failures to others who have sufficient time and experience to assess the evidence and report on it." "Accountability obliges you to be able to demonstrate that success to third parties....and hence that you are in fact successful" (Scriven, 1994, p. 159). O'Neill and others (e.g., Didau, 2020) see that the current accountability climate is based on a deficit model where performance is seen as an error and blamed. This approach to accountability restricts rather than motivates or supports teachers. So, too, when student test scores were tied to teacher evaluation, and ultimately a reward (merit) or punishment (dismissal), evaluation became even more dysfunctional than it had already become.

Elsewhere, I have argued the many reasons why teacher evaluation is complicated and dysfunctional (Hazi, 2019, 2022a, 2022b). Here, I highlight one: it no longer serves its formative purpose (Hazi, 2022a). Perhaps it is that teachers have limited say in what information would be helpful for their improvement. Teachers are accustomed to administrators presenting them with standardized test scores. Such test scores are presented as numbers that are difficult to understand and fail to indicate what teachers should do to improve (Ebbeler et al., 2017). Administrators also present their ratings of behavior rather than evidence. Both tend to be out of context and unrelated to the lesson, subject, grade level, and student ability.

Instead, we might consider that principals use teacher evaluation to triage teachers in need of improvement and dismissal. For those teachers requiring improvement, principals can help match them with one of many promising practices within a system of improvement. For those requiring dismissal, principals, with the help of specialists, can corroborate and then document irremediable behaviors. Still, many teachers may want to work with the principal or another option where they can study their practice.

The purpose of this chapter is to describe an example of a system of intelligent accountability that helps teachers work toward improvement by studying their practice. Such a system can help teachers account for their practice to other teachers and, perhaps in time, to the students and parents they serve. While there are many promising practices of instructional improvement, three that can fit within this system are described here. They are peer-assisted self-evaluation, lesson study, and instructional rounds. The author draws from the scholarship of intelligent accountability and evidence literacy, in addition to that of the promising practices. Corbett Prep, an independent day school, is offered as a case to illustrate a place where intelligent accountability can exist. Here, the teachers' team plans, teaches, and assesses instruction. It is also where administrators don't evaluate teachers and deliver feedback, yet everyone knows if they "fit" (Hazi, 2023a).

PRINCIPLES OF INTELLIGENT ACCOUNTABILITY

Intelligent accountability is "a system of responsibilities where educators co-create and participate in a public process to account for their practice with evidence to judge it" (Hazi, 2024a, p. 92). Here, the systems of accountability and professional learning intersect and are a way for principals to transform and improve both individuals and groups of teachers. The responsibility of principals and supervisors is to work with stakeholders to develop, facilitate, and monitor a system to ensure its success in a culture that supports it.

While I have described the process in more detail elsewhere (Hazi, 2024b), the general goal is to study aspects of one's teaching framed within the promising practice of peer-supported self-evaluation, to be later described in more detail. "Each teacher engages in continuous cycles of goal setting, classroom experimentation, and public reflection on learnings, where the community challenges teachers to take the next steps to even more experiential learning and subsequent growth" (p. 100). This inquiry process requires an evaluative mindset and evidence literacy. Evidence literacy includes the skill to identify, collect, and interpret evidence to transform it into useable knowledge to understand and act upon one's practice. Several principles guide the development of this process. Elsewhere, I have written about them in detail (Hazi, 2024a), but in brief, they involve participation that is voluntary, where teachers focus on learning and share that learning within a community.

Teachers can participate instead of being isolated and individualistic and are first accountable to a community of like-minded peers (Hargreaves, 1994). This system allows teachers to study their practice and disclose their mistakes and weaknesses in a safe place. Teachers must find and invent "ways to put aside the pretensions and fears that keep most teachers behind closed doors" (McDonald, 1992, p. 12). "What happens on this deeper level is that the uncertainties that elude the grasp of private introspection… become group problems. The conversation they provoke amplifies individual interpretation and builds a sense of professional community" (p. 12). The community of teachers supports and helps each other to collect, share, and publicly reflect on evidence. This public sharing is not a confessional of incompetence but a safe space where teachers can disclose what troubles them about a student, group, technique, or process and where teachers provide another set of eyes to confirm or challenge evidence and its interpretation and come to insights through experimentation and reflection.

THE CASE OF CORBETT PREP

Corbett Preparatory is a unique PreK through 8th-grade school where teachers learn and continuously improve. It has the infrastructure that can support a system of intelligent accountability: a culture that supports teacher learning, and multiple forms of teaming with time for collaboration. In this section, Corbett Prep is described highlighting its infrastructure, then three promising practices are offered to further the aims of intelligent accountability.

Corbett Prep is a nonprofit, independent day school founded in 1968 by two teachers and supported by special donors and the community (Hazi, 2023a). Accredited by the Florida Council of Independent Schools (2021),

Corbett is accountable to its communities and accrediting body, but with more discretion and less regulation than is in public schools. Here, administrators can flexibly use time and teachers who are trusted professionals involved in most aspects of the school's decision-making. It's a place where school is exciting, mistakes are opportunities to improve, and its 550 students experience active learning, as its opening day Facebook post for August 14, 2024 reports: "Classes performed magical experiments, embarked on scavenger hunts, released butterflies, launched rockets, solved Escape Room mysteries, played team building games and unleashed their creativity in special projects" (https://www.facebook.com/CorbettPrep/).

Corbett has a unique environment for its 90 staff who love learning and go the extra mile so children can learn and where administrators make the job of teaching easier. Some teachers have been there for over twenty-five years, as had one of its early headmasters who organized teachers in teams for instruction and supported them with professional development and time for meetings embedded in the school day. New teachers receive five days of orientation prior to the start of school and are placed in a team whose members participate in their interviews. Professional development is guided by research-based learning strategies, programs recognized by national educational associations, and "best practices" (Cohen, 2003). Teachers are responsible for curriculum and instructional initiatives by investigating them, attending workshops, making modifications, and evaluating their success.

The administrators at Corbett Prep attribute their school's success, innovations, and many awards to teaming, which was initiated by one of its early headmasters, influenced by the work of supervision scholar Robert Anderson. Teaming drives the school schedule, its professional development, and teacher collaboration, which, in turn, drives the school's continuous improvement.

Anderson (2023) began writing about teaming at Harvard University in the 1950s and 1960s. At that time, team teaching had been promoted along with non-gradedness to promote professional flexibility and resources for teaching in the learning environment. It became an alternative to the age-graded grouping of students, who were expected to function academically within the same grade level, and where teachers taught standardized curriculum in self-contained classrooms, independent of their colleagues.

According to Anderson (2023), teams of 4–6 elementary and middle school teachers share responsibilities for teaching multi-age groups of children. Teaming provides professional company, professional development, and induction for those newly hired teachers. While it became popular in places such as Corbett, teachers elsewhere were resistant because they lost their privacy and independence and could not ignore the difficult student or difficult-to-teach curriculum. With teaming, teachers can flexibly teach individuals and small groups to meet student needs best and to teach to their strengths while observing other teachers do the same.

At Corbett, teaming takes many forms including vertical (subject), horizontal (grade), teacher, leadership, and special event/purpose teams. "Corbett has various levels of teams that combine and recombine within and across grade levels, within and across subjects and divisions, and within and outside of the school. Corbett Prep teams have developed relationships with teachers in other countries" (Hazi, 2023a, p. 97).

Administrators protect teacher time at Corbett. Meetings are scheduled at the beginning of the school year and occur during, before and after the school day, ranging from 45 to 90 minutes. All teachers have a daily planning period of 60 minutes, time every Tuesday from 3–5:00 for workshops and meetings, one-half day monthly for in-service, and released time for professional conferences throughout the school year. Teachers have amazing learning and travel opportunities as this August 7, 2024 Facebook post reports:

Three of our amazing educators kicked off their summer with an incredible journey through Europe to visit international educational institutions and experience learning ... [at] world-renowned schools and UNESCO sites in Spain, Switzerland, Germany, France and the Netherlands!

The goal of the trip was to strengthen connections and establish partnerships with schools in parts of Europe. The teachers said the journey was truly eye-opening, offering a wealth of insights into educational practices and cultures. The visits have strengthened Corbett Prep's commitment to fostering a learning environment that embraces international perspectives as well as innovative teaching methodologies. (https://www.facebook.com/CorbettPrep/).

Teaming in its many forms has been recently rediscovered in the US Team teaching, a central component of a schoolwide improvement strategy, has been successfully used in high-poverty urban schools, where principals protect team time, attend their meetings, and support teachers across the school (Johnson, 2019). While teaming takes considerable time, teachers were enthusiastic, had less stress, and made their job more rewarding: "Teachers feel like they can go to somebody and ask questions or admit if they're struggling with something and get support from their coworkers" (Johnson et al., 2016, p. 25). In these schools teaming "improved the quality of lessons and eased the burden of daily planning" (p. 26). Teaming helps in induction when new teachers are assigned to a team of veterans, in staffing in special education, and in developing your multidisciplinary courses (Zalaznick, 2022). Some also saw how pre-established teaming helped teachers pivot quickly to plan remote instruction and navigate the pandemic so that students could attend synchronous virtual sessions in the morning and live classes such as fitness, tutoring, and enrichment in the afternoon (Johnson, 2021).

Elsewhere, universities have become involved in teaming with preservice and inservice teachers. One example is *The Next Education Workforce* at Arizona State University. Here, Title I specialists, special educators, special subject teachers, and resident teachers plan, monitor, and teach public school students who need extra attention. In preliminary results, teachers are more likely to remain at their school and within teaching for five years, to recommend teaching to a friend, and to have higher evaluation ratings (Laski, 2024). Another initiative in 55 school systems in 10 states, Public Impact's *Opportunity Culture*, identifies excellent teachers to become multi-classroom leaders to mentor teams of educators on how to plan, co-teach, coach and analyze student data (Chen & Banchero, 2022). In preliminary results, teacher recruitment and retention have improved and students show on average gains of an extra one-half year of learning in subjects such as reading and math (Public Impact, 2024).

At Corbett Prep, teachers are accountable to members of their team(s) daily. The teacher team will plan, teach, and assess instruction. One teacher said that in the public schools, she was isolated and "worked on an island," but here, she enjoys teaming:

> 'Love having a partner to work with. I spend more time with her than with my own husband and children. We fight like we're a married couple.' …Another said, 'We complement each other. No one is the leader. Everyone takes leadership on different parts based on what they do best. I'm not as good alone, as the 3 of us together.' Still, another said, 'It's like a think tank where everyone actively shares. Everyone has respect for each other. Everyone has everyone else's back. We help each other.' (Hazi, 2023a, p. 98)

Teachers were adamant that they were not evaluated:

> 'Teacher evaluation' by this name does *not* exist at Corbett Prep, yet teachers and administrators experience it as whether they "fit." In what I call the "culture of fit," teachers are "kept in-check, "coached," and "micro-analyzed" by other teachers. Teachers describe it as a "mindset" or "perspective" and the "Olympic Mentality." "Joyce [the headmaster] would say it's the best getting better,' said one teacher, 'standing on the shoulders of those who've come before us.' Most importantly, teachers come to understand whether they belong at this school. (p. 103)

Administrators do observe and provide written feedback. However, they see their rightful value when they hire teachers based on team needs, protect team time, attend their meetings, support teachers, and listen to their complaints. They try to place the weaker teachers where they would fit in another team or role before encouraging them to leave the school and want teachers to share a "wow moment" with the whole faculty (Hazi, 2023a).

Two teachers sum up the school culture that supports them in the following:

> 'I need to be supported by my colleagues and management and be allowed to support them, listened to, invited to give my opinions, given the authority to do things and then allowed to do them. Give and receive constructive advice, be mentored, and trusted to mentor....'Trust is felt everywhere at Corbett. I have autonomy over my classroom, am able to lead events, and my opinions are listened to and valued. I am greeted with a smile. My principal has an open-door policy—she will make time to meet with me at a moment's notice, and if not then, she will schedule a time that is usually the same day.' (p. 105)

Teaming and time for collaborations are essential to the infrastructure at Corbett Preparatory, an independent day school. Teachers feel trusted and supported as the professionals they are. When asked they might not claim it, but from the outside looking in, intelligent accountability exists here. While it did not happen over night, it took many years to find and accumulate the existing staff, and for those "weaker links" to recognize they did not "fit" and leave. Can teaming exist elsewhere? With other examples, it appears possible where leaders work around obstacles, see the value, trust teachers and involve them in decision making, and have the will to avoid a dysfunctional system of accountability.

Promising Strategies

Instructional improvement is complicated and is more than a principal delivering feedback to teachers. It requires providing multiple options so that teachers can select a promising strategy that meets their needs. A *promising strategy*, according to Darling-Hammond et al. (2009), is one that has some evidence of impact but "are not yet confirmed by a solid body of evidence, and the jury remains out as to their effectiveness or conditions under which they are most likely to be effective" (p. 12). Elsewhere I have described many as has Glanz (2024),[1] but here I focus on three: peer-assisted self-evaluation, lesson study, and instructional rounds. These three strategies can fit within Corbett Prep, fully involve teachers in studying their practice, generate new knowledge about practice, and individually and collectively promote teacher learning. A brief description of each is presented here with some key references so readers might find more.

Peer-assisted self-evaluation: "[S]elf-evaluation is the most common of all forms of teacher evaluation" but goes unnoticed because it's done informally (Airasian & Gullickson, 2006, p. 6). It is "a process in which teachers make judgments about the adequacy and effectiveness of their own knowledge, performance, beliefs, and effects for the purpose of self-improvement" (p. 186). It has "historically...been of little value. Most dismiss it as a strategy of self-improvement that is fraught with problems," (Barber, 1991, p. 216) but has been recently rediscovered for professional development.

Its purpose is formative. "A problem or question about practice arises from a sense of discomfort, curiosity, or a desire to change" (Airasian & Gullickson, 2006, p. 3). The teacher collects, interprets, and judges evidence against criteria then decides on the professional development activities warranted. Evidence can include checklists, student surveys, student work, journaling, videotaped lessons, and peer observations. It relates to reflection and inquiry but differs in that teachers make decisions about the evidence, how it is collected, and how it is judged in advance. Barriers include lack of time, vague plans, overlooking evidence, and oversimplified explanations. For these reasons, peers can (and should) assist in its planning, evidence collection, and interpretation. Collaboration with peers, especially to establish criteria, can result in a common understanding and vocabulary to talk about good teaching.

Corbett Prep's teachers most likely informally self-evaluate when debriefing lessons. However, teams could formalize this practice by allowing teachers to set content and pedagogical goals for individual (or team) improvement, collecting and discussing evidence, and then setting new goals that would parallel their teaching plans. While this would add more time at the onset, it might be a way for teams to evolve where evaluation would become less time-consuming naturally. This could also be done periodically when a unit or grading period naturally ends.

Instructional Rounds: While there are many versions of instructional rounds (e.g., City et al., 2010; Elmore, 2007; Marzano, 2021), most involve a school-based team of teachers that observe a lesson around a problem of practice or standards of teaching for a fixed amount of time, debrief and discuss teaching. It is a collaborative learning model where participants observe in classrooms and co-construct knowledge about teaching practices (City et al., 2010). It's an adaption of medical rounds that develop physicians' diagnostic and treatment practice where groups of interns and their attending physicians visit patients, observe and discuss evidence. Observers decide "in advance what to observe, how to observe, and ... how to talk about what is seen" (City et al., 2010, pp. 85–86). The evidence gives teachers the basis for common conversation and "the consensus view" of powerful teacher learning (Elmore, 2004). Its use in teacher education is considered "more recent" and supported by the concepts of reflection and inquiry, critical reflection and deliberation, and communities of practice (Goodwin et al., 2015).

While research is "still in its infancy" and is needed to determine if instructional rounds can lead to increased student achievement, there are some encouraging results for preservice teacher learning. Instructional rounds helped preservice teachers to develop confidence and agency, see a wider range of practices, to look beyond their initial concerns about classroom management to classroom culture and pedagogical approaches, and to consider some of their previously unexamined assumptions about students who fell through the cracks (Lee, 2015; also see for a special issue). Inservice teachers report increased morale and a sense of recognition.

Teachers need to ensure that knowledgeable others are involved in the process as co-learners. Furthermore, they would need to allow more time for reflection, encourage multiple and competing definitions of good teaching, and move the discussion beyond a "culture of niceness" (Elmore, 2007) and "contrived collegiality" (Hargreaves, 2010).

Lesson Study: Lesson study, originating in Japan in the 19th century and spreading internationally and in the US since 1999, is a collaborative study of live classroom lessons (Lewis et al., 2006). It is considered a "traveling reform," a model of excellent practice borrowed from other countries (Godfrey et al., 2019).

Lesson study in Japan is unique in that teachers initiate it and involve watching a live lesson. The Japanese have four types of lesson study with an emphasis on public sharing: school-wide in grade levels, district-level focused on a subject(s), national-level with a national school opening up participation to thousands of educators, and association-sponsored to examine a live research-based lesson (see Lee, 2015). Lesson Study is about collective practice over time, where lessons are selected, planned, observed and discussed within contexts of its class, students, curriculum unit, and school to determine the lesson's impact on student learning. The goal of Japanese educators is to observe as many lessons as possible which could amount to 100 lessons a year.

> Lesson Study focuses on helping teachers to develop the eyes to see children and how they respond and learn during research lessons. Observers in Lesson Study do not sit at the back of the classrooms as all they would see from that vantage point are the backs of students' heads but rather they stand at the corners and sides observing the students' faces, postures and body language. (Lee, 2015, p. 103)

In the US, mathematics teachers were among the first to use data to study a mathematical lesson in its context, revise it, and then re-teach it. Since its introduction by Stigler and Hiebert (2017) in the US, in a matter of 4 years, it has appeared in 335 US schools in 32 states and been the subject of dozens of conferences, reports, and published articles that describe and give advice on conducting (Lewis et al., 2006). It has rapidly proliferated since that time with twice as many schools and as many as 105 universities participating (Cheung & Wong, 2013). While some characterize it as an "immature innovation" requiring study with randomized trials, it has been an accepted practice for over a century in Japan, with "instructional knowledge accumulate[ing] through progressive advances in research lessons taught in various local contexts across Japan, rather than through large-scale or centralized studies" (Lewis et al., 2006, p. 6). Therefore, "lesson study thus provides a professional knowledge base about teaching that is public, shareable, and verifiable" (p. 7)

Its goal is to help teachers learn– not just to produce a great lesson (Heibert & Stigler, 2016; Stigler & Hiebert, 2016). The lesson study can help make the workings of a lesson explicit, where teachers can discuss student thinking and learning, lesson content, and then try the instruction they hypothesize is most effective. In addition to a lesson, the focus of inquiry can be a student, a group of students, a classroom routine, a series of lessons, a unit, a curriculum, a program, or any system.

Its scholarship consists of literature reviews or theory-based articles, while its research includes case reports with limited studies of interventions or validated outcomes. Despite these limitations, Cheung and Wong (2013) found positive evidence supporting its benefits to teachers, students, and both. Godfrey et al. (2019) found that in their review of 36 empirical studies, teachers enjoyed lesson study, subject content knowledge, pedagogy, and confidence changed, and teachers reported that student learning improved.

Lesson study is promoted by the American Federation of Teachers (2024), a national teachers union, as professional development that focuses on teaching and where "the success of a lesson study is measured in teachers' learning, and not the perfection of a lesson. That better lessons are created is a secondary byproduct of the process, but not its primary goal" (AFT, 2024, para 2). Lesson study groups are found in schools in Rochester, N.Y., Volusia County, Fla., Scranton, Pa., and Chicago, Ill., and special projects at the University of Wisconsin-La Crosse and Mills College in California.

CONCLUSION

These three promising practices focus on teacher learning and intelligent accountability. Teacher learning has been missing from most US reforms and accountability initiatives. However, suppose educators and policymakers want quality teaching. In that case, their efforts must promote teacher learning with professional development, provide time in the school day, and trust teachers to be the professionals they aspire to be.

CASE STUDY

Use school as the case, and reflect on these points.

REFLECTIONS ON THE CASE

- Select one or more of the promising practices presented above (or those listed in footnote 1) to investigate further. Why does this promising practice have the potential to fit at your school? What supports (i.e., time during the school day, online platforms, substitutes, etc.) would be needed to succeed?
- Using Corbett Prep (or your own school) as the case context, describe what you would do to prepare it for this practice? What infrastructure exists that will support it? What changes would have to occur with its accountability system to succeed? What challenges do you anticipate in its implementation?
- I have assumed, but not made explicit, that professional development would accompany any promising practice. What are the qualities of effective professional development (e.g., Gore et al. 2021 or the *Learning Forward* website), and what professional development would you provide on one of the promising practices, pointing out these characteristics?

NOTE

1. Hazi (2023b) includes: formative assessment, National Board Certification, professional development, coaching, professional learning communities, mentoring, and teacher advice networks. Glanz (2024) lists clinical supervision, demonstration lessons and videotaping, intervisitations, peer coaching, action research, book studies, reflective journaling, lesson studies, and instructional rounds..

REFERENCES

Airasian, P., & Gullickson, A. (2006). Teacher self-evaluation. In J. Stronge (Ed.), *Evaluating teaching: A guide to current thinking and best practice* (2nd ed., pp. 186–211). Corwin Press.
American Federation of Teachers (AFT). (2024). *AFT, "What is lesson study?* https://www.aft.org/education/well-prepared-and-supported-school-staff/what-lesson-study
Anderson, R. (2023). The beginnings of collaboration schools: Team teaching and multi-age grouping. In K. J. Snyder & K. M. Snyder (Eds.), *Systems thinking for sustainable schooling: A mindshift for educators to lead and achieve quality in schools.* Rowman & Littlefield.
Barber, L. (1991). Self-assessment. In L. Darling-Hammond & J. Millman (Eds.), *Handbook of teacher evaluation* (pp. 216–228). Sage Publications.
Chen, I., & Banchero, S. (2022). It's time to rethink the 'one teacher, one classroom' model. *Education Week.* https://www.edweek.org/teaching-learning/opinion-its-time-to-rethink-one-teacher-one-classroom-model

Cheung, W., & Wong, W. (2013). Does lesson study work? A systematic review on the effects of lesson study and learning study on teachers and students. *International Journal for Lesson and Learning Studies, 3*(2), 137–149. https://doi.org/10.1108/IJLLS-05-2013-0024

City, E., Elmore, R., Fiarman, S., & Teitel, L. (2010). *Instructional rounds in education: A network approach to improving teaching and learning.* Harvard Education Press.

Darling-Hammond, L., Wei, R. C., Andree, A., Richardson, N., & Orphanos, S. (2009, February). *Professional learning in the learning profession: A status report on teacher development in the United States and abroad.* National Staff Development Council and The School Redesign Network. https://edpolicy.stanford.edu/sites/default/files/publications/professional-learning-learning-profession-status-report-teacher-development-us-and-abroad.pdf

Didau, D. (2020). *Intelligent accountability: Creating the conditions for teachers to thrive.* John Catt.

Ebbeler, J., Poortman, C., Schildkamp, K., & Pieters, J. (2017). The effects of a data use intervention on educators' satisfaction and data literacy. *Educational Assessment, Evaluation Accountability, 29,* 83–105. https://doi.org/10.1007/s11092-016-9251-z

Elmore, R. F. (2004). *School reform from the inside out: Policy, practice and performance.* Harvard Education Press.

Elmore, R. F. (2007). Professional networks and school improvement. *School Administrator, 64*(4), 20–24.

Florida Council of Independent Schools (FCIS). (2021. June). *FCIS manual for evaluation and accreditation.* https://www.rcis.org/accreditation/resources-for-schools

Glanz, J. (2024). *Creating a culture of excellence: A school leader's guide to best practices in teaching, curriculum, professional development, supervision, and evaluation.* Rowman & Littlefield.

Godfrey, D., Seleznyov, A., Anders, J., Wollaston, N., & Barrera-Pedemonte, F. (2019). A developmental evaluation approach to lesson study: Exploring the impact of lesson study in London schools. *Professional Development in Education, 45*(2), 325–340. https://doi.org/10.1080/19415257.2018.1474488

Goodwin, A., Prete, T., Reagan, E., & Roegman, R. (2015). A closer look at the practice and impact of rounds. *International Journal of Educational Research, 73,* 37–43. https://doi.org/10.1016/j.ijer.2015.06.006

Gore, J., Miller, A., Fray, L., Harris, J., & Prieto, E. (2021). Improving student achievement through professional development: Results from a randomized controlled trial of quality teaching rounds. *Teaching and Teacher Education, 101.* https://doi.org/10.1016/j.tate.2021.103297

Hargreaves, A. (1994). The new professionalism: The synthesis of professional and institutional development. *Teaching and Teacher Education, 10*(4), 423–438. https://doi.org/10.1016/0742-051X(94)90023-X

Hargreaves, A. (2010). Presentism, individualism and conservatism: The legacy of Dan Lortie's Schoolteacher: A sociological study. *Curriculum Inquiry, 40,* 143–153. https://doi.org/10.1111/j.1467-873X.2009.00472.x

Hazi, H. M. (2019). Coming to understand the wicked problem of teacher evaluation. In S. Zepeda & J. Ponticell (Eds.), *Handbook of supervision* (pp. 183–207). Wiley Blackwell Publishing. https://doi.org/10.1002/9781119128304.ch8

Hazi, H. M. (2022a). Reconsidering the dual purposes of teacher evaluation. *Teachers and Teaching: Theory and Practice*, 1–15. https://doi.org/10.1080/13540602.2022.2103533

Hazi, H. M. (2022b). The restrictive concepts of teacher evaluation and their discourse communities. *Journal of Educational Supervision, 5*(1), 47–67. https://doi.org/10.31045/jes.5.1.3

Hazi, H. M. (2023a). (Re)imagined teacher learning and improvement with systems thinking: The case of Corbett Prep and its "culture of fit.". In K. M. Snyder & K. J. Snyder (Eds.), *Regenerating schools as living systems: Success stories of systems thinking in action* (pp. 99–108). Rowman & Littlefield.

Hazi, H. M. (2023b). Promising supervisory theories and strategies for instructional improvement. In A. Lavigne & M. L. Derrington (Eds.), *Actional feedback to PK-12 teachers* (pp. 11–22). Rowman & Littlefield.

Hazi, H. M. (2024a). Intelligent accountability: Principles for practice. In H. Hazi & M. Piantanida (Eds.), *Snapshots of instructional supervision: Reflections of scholars in the field* (pp. 91–102). Learning Moments Press.

Hazi, H. M. (2024b). Rethinking teacher evaluation as professional development for culturally responsive pedagogy. In I. Mette, D. Cormier, & Y. Oliveras-Ortiz (Eds.), *Culturally responsive supervision* (pp. 97–111). Teachers College Press.

Hiebert, J., & Stigler, J. W. (2017). Teaching versus teachers as a lever for change: Comparing a Japanese and a U.S. perspective on improving instruction. *Educational Researcher, 46*(4), 169–176. https://journals.sagepub.com/doi/abs/10.3102/0013189X17711899?journalCode=edra

Johnson, S. (2019). *Where teachers thrive: Organizing schools for success.* Harvard Education Press.

Johnson, S. (2021, August 30). Why teacher teams are more critical than ever. *Educational Leadership.* https://www.ascd.org/el/articles/why-teacher-teams-are-more-critical-than-ever

Johnson, S. M., Reinhorn, S., & Simon, N. (2016). Team work: Time well spent. *Educational Leadership, 73*(8), 24–29. https://www.ascd.org/el/articles/team-work-time-well-spent

Laski, M. (2024, May). *Early evidence of improved educator outcomes in next education workforce.* Arizona State University Center on Reinvention Public Education. https://crpe.org/early-evidence-of-improved-educator-outcomes-in-next-education-workforcetm-models/#:~:text=Key%20Findings%3A,recommend%20teaching%20to%20a%20friend

Lee, C. K.-E. (2015). Examining education rounds through the lens of lesson study. *International Journal of Educational Research, 73,* 100–106. https://doi.org/10.1016/j.ijer.2015.07.001

Lewis, C., Perry, R., & Murata, A. (2006). How should research contribute to instructional improvement: The case of lesson study. *Educational Researcher, 35*(3), 3–14. https://journals.sagepub.com/doi/10.3102/0013189X035003003

Marzano, R. (2021). The art & science of teaching: Making the most of instructional rounds. *Educational Leadership, 68*(5). https://ascd.org/el/articles/making-the-most-of-instructional-rounds

McDonald, J. (1992). *Teaching: making sense of an uncertain craft.* Teachers College Press.

Noddings, N. (2007). *When school reform goes wrong.* Teachers College Press.

O'Neill, O. (2002). *A question of trust: The BBC Reith lectures 2002.* Cambridge University Press.

O'Neill, O. (2013). Intelligent accountability in education. *Oxford Review of Education, 39*(1), 4–16. https://doi.org/10.1080/03054985.2013.764761

Public Impact. (2024). *Research shows results: Opportunity culture teams lead to strong student learning gains, research shows.* https://www.opportunityculture.org/research/

Scriven, M. (1994). Duties of a teacher. *Journal of Personnel Evaluation in Education, 8*(2), 151–184. https://doi.org/10.1007/BF00972261

Stigler, J. W., & Hiebert, J. (2016). Lesson study, improvement, and the importing of cultural routines. *ZDM Mathematics Education, 48*, 581–587. https://link.springer.com/article/10.1007/s11858-016-0787-7

Zalaznick, M. (2022, September 21). *Can the increasingly popular team-teaching models reenergize the profession?* District Administration. https://districtadministration.com/team-teaching-co-teaching-re-energize-k-12-education/

CHAPTER 7

SHIFTING PARADIGMS IN PRINCIPAL LEADERSHIP: ENTREPRENEURIAL MIDDLE LEADER AMIDST TRANSFORMATIONAL CHANGE

Chun Sing Maxwell Ho
Education University, Hong Kong

ABSTRACT

Chun Sing Maxwell Ho, in Chapter 7, discusses middle school leaders as instrumental in actualizing transformational leadership through entrepreneurial action. These leaders create a vision, but the vision is actually challenging, given various organizational constraints and challenges. The paper focuses on the efforts of a middle school principal to convert visionary principles into concrete, actionable outcomes that nurture environments ripe for middle leaders and school improvement. The study offers a wealth of insights for transformational leadership at the middle school level in transforming otherwise traditional organizational policies and practices into actionable strategies and thoughtful reflections on nurturing a culture of innovation and adaptability. By dissecting the experiences of middle leaders who have successfully navigated the transition from conceptual frameworks to tangible educational outcomes, the chapter provides strategies to equip school leaders with the knowledge to empower their teams, advocate for resourceful problem-solving, and champion a collaborative approach to leadership.

Keywords: Middle school leadership; reforming middle schools; school culture; student outcomes; middle schools; educational outcomes

---

Prefocus Guiding Questions

- *What do you know about teacher leadership?*
- *What is the difference between an "entrepreneurial teacher" and a "teacher leader"?*
- *Consider your school situation and chart the changes necessary to improve student learning, and how might you create positive change?*

INTRODUCTION

In response to emerging trends such as digital learning platforms, personalized education, and global competence requirements—integral to the continuously evolving educational landscape—schools are increasingly required to adopt innovative approaches for improvement (Fullan, 2023). This demand for continual renewal and adaptation has highlighted the critical role of entrepreneurial teacher leaders in driving school improvement (Ho et al., 2022). These leaders excel in promoting and implementing innovative practices across their schools, effectively inspiring their peers (Davis, 2023). Research on entrepreneurial behavior among teacher leaders has demonstrated their significant impact in identifying and leveraging opportunities for innovation. They cultivate communities of practice that support the widespread adoption and sustainability of innovative strategies, underscoring that effective school improvement substantially depends on the entrepreneurial initiatives of these leaders (Ho et al., 2020, 2024; Joensuu-Salo et al., 2021). As they navigate challenges and steer their teams toward embracing change, their role in achieving educational excellence becomes increasingly crucial (Zhao et al., 2022).

Parenthetically, the notion of teacher leadership is present in the research literature (Lovett, 2023). What is the difference between "entrepreneurial teachers" and "teacher leaders," a term for lead teachers that became popular ten years ago? The distinctions between "entrepreneurial teachers" and "teacher leaders" are nuanced and revolve around the scope of their roles and the nature of their contributions to educational settings.

Entrepreneurial Teachers: This term broadly encompasses educators at various levels, including classroom teachers, subject heads, and assistant principals, who exhibit Teacher Entrepreneurial Behaviors. These behaviors include innovation, risk-taking, and proactive engagement in school activities beyond traditional teaching duties. Formal leadership titles do not define entrepreneurial teachers but emerge through their actions and initiatives demonstrating entrepreneurial qualities. They often play crucial roles in introducing and driving change within their schools, fostering a culture of innovation. While they may not always hold formal leadership positions, their impact often propels them into such roles over time.

Teacher Leaders: This is a broader category that includes any educator who takes on leadership responsibilities, whether in curriculum development, mentoring, administrative roles, or policy influence. Teacher leaders may or may not exhibit entrepreneurial behaviors. Their leadership can manifest through various forms, including but not limited to guiding peers, leading professional development, or managing teams. 'teacher leaders' encompass a wider range of leadership styles and responsibilities than 'entrepreneurial teachers.'

In essence, while all entrepreneurial teachers have the potential to become teacher leaders, not all teacher leaders necessarily engage in entrepreneurial activities. The role of entrepreneurial teachers, characterized by their innovative and proactive nature, serves as a dynamic subset within the broader teacher leadership framework.

Transformational principals, who adopt leadership practices that significantly boost the motivation and capacity of teacher leaders to pursue and implement entrepreneurial initiatives, play a crucial role in fostering an environment conducive to innovation and leadership (Eyal & Kark, 2004; Ho et al., 2023a). However, as new principals come into office, the environment these leaders create also changes (Fusarelli et al., 2018). These changes in principal behavior can profoundly influence the scope and direction of the entrepreneurial activities undertaken by teacher leaders. Despite the importance of this dynamic, research on how teacher leaders navigate these evolving leadership landscapes remains limited. This gap underscores a critical challenge in educational innovation—its sustainability amid shifting principal leadership (Dimmock & Yong Tan, 2013). Therefore, this chapter aims to unveil the strategies entrepreneurial leaders employ to translate visionary principles into concrete, actionable outcomes that align with the original direction of entrepreneurial teachers.

This chapter provides theoretical insights into the adaptability and resilience of middle leaders within educational settings, enriching the body of knowledge on how these leaders adjust their strategies to align with new leadership visions and sustain innovative momentum. Practically, the findings offer strategic guidance for both incoming and outgoing school principals, highlighting how to foster an environment that nurtures sustainable entrepreneurial initiatives. This chapter aids in maintaining and enhancing innovative projects, ensuring that schools can effectively respond to leadership transitions while continuing to foster a culture of innovation.

LITERATURE REVIEW

Transformational Leadership

Transformational leadership is a leadership style where leaders inspire and motivate their followers to achieve extraordinary outcomes, fostering an environment rich in trust and innovation (Bass, 1985). It is distinguished by the collaborative efforts of leaders and their followers to recognize and implement necessary changes, all guided by a compelling, shared vision (Leithwood et al., 2021). Transformational leaders inspire followers to pursue ambitious goals, develop new skills, and enhance performance through strategic guidance and consistent monitoring (Jolanta, 2013; Kroth & Boverie, 2009). Typically, four major characteristics define this leadership approach.

Idealized influence is fundamental to this style, where leaders act as charismatic role models who demonstrate integrity and trustworthiness, inspiring followers to emulate their values and behaviors (Bass & Riggio, 2006; Fitzgerald & Schutte, 2010). Transformational leaders also provide individualized consideration, offering personalized support and understanding the diverse cultural dynamics within their teams (Walker & Riordan, 2010). They maintain a robust and inspiring vision, modeling behaviors that align with organizational goals (Berkovich, 2016). Another key component is intellectual stimulation, where leaders challenge conventional thinking and encourage creative problem-solving by adapting organizational structures, clearing obstacles, and provisioning resources (Kotter, 2012). This holistic approach not only fosters an environment of continuous improvement and innovation but also cultivates a leadership culture that thrives on ethical standards and shared success.

Transformational leadership profoundly influences teachers by creating an environment that fosters teachers' professional growth and collaboration (Eyal & Kark, 2004). Through open communication and trust, transformational leaders unify the teaching staff, enhancing their effectiveness and cohesiveness (Berkovich, 2016). This leadership style encourages teachers to adopt innovative teaching strategies and technologies and actively supports their exploration, improving learning outcomes (Li & Liu, 2022). Furthermore, by offering individualized consideration, transformational leaders address each teacher's unique professional needs and aspirations, thereby increasing job satisfaction and retention (Kılınç et al., 2024).

Transformational leadership fosters entrepreneurial behavior in employees, creating environments ripe for innovation and proactive engagement (Jensen & Luthans, 2006; Leitch & Volery, 2017). This style of leadership not only enhances a firm's entrepreneurial orientation but boosts overall performance by encouraging risk-taking and continuous innovation (Engelen et al., 2015). Furthermore, transformational leadership is pivotal in innovation management, propelling organizations toward sustained growth and enhanced competitiveness (Fontana & Musa, 2017). Such leaders inspire teachers to embrace change in educational settings, improving school performance through increased innovation and adaptability (Leithwood, 2001). Eyal and Kark (2004) expand on this by demonstrating how transformational leadership specifically influences the adoption of entrepreneurial behaviors among teachers, which drives significant school change.

Entrepreneurial Teacher Leaders

Entrepreneurial teacher leaders are a distinct subset of teacher leaders who embody the behaviors of entrepreneurs within the school setting (Ho et al., 2023b). Unlike conventional teacher leaders, who may focus primarily on instructional leadership and curriculum development, entrepreneurial teacher leaders engage in behaviors that extend beyond the classroom to initiate and manage innovative educational projects (Ho et al., 2021; Van Dam et al., 2010). These individuals exhibit Teacher Entrepreneurial Behavior Teacher Entrepreneurial Behaviors, characterized by advocating for new and innovative practices, seeking and managing resources effectively, mitigating risks associated with new initiatives, and building consensus while maintaining a respectful and inclusive approach (Chand & Amin-Choudhury, 2006; Ho et al., 2021; Martin et al., 2018). This multifaceted behavior enables them to act as agents of change who can navigate and lead complex transformations within educational institutions. By leveraging their entrepreneurial skills, these leaders can implement strategies that significantly enhance teaching and learning outcomes (Zhao et al., 2022).

Entrepreneurial teacher leaders are often at the forefront of educational innovation, leading initiatives that can transform school cultures, improve student engagement and learning outcomes, and increase the effectiveness of teaching practices (Ho et al., 2021). Their ability to think creatively and manage resources strategically allows them to implement sustainable changes that positively impact the entire school community (Joensuu-Salo et al., 2021). Practically, they often create or revise curricula to serve as channels for initiating these innovative practices, directly influencing the educational framework (Ho et al., 2024; Zappe et al., 2021). Additionally, entrepreneurial teacher leaders inspire other educators to embrace change by fostering innovation and open-mindedness, multiplying their impact and driving widespread educational reform (Ho et al., 2020; Hanson, 2017).

Impact of Leadership Transition on School

The arrival of a new principal in a school can significantly influence the ongoing processes and cultural dynamics established under former leadership.

When transformational leaders are replaced, it often leads to a disruptive phase within the organization (Mattar, 2020). Such changes can be stressful for subordinates due to the potential loss of a transformational leader. As a new principal steps in, the school may undergo profound changes that render it nearly unrecognizable compared to its former state, challenging the adaptability and resilience of both staff and students (Shoho & Barnett, 2010). This stress is compounded by transformational change, necessitating a radical shift in organizational operations.

Moreover, transitioning to a new principal can evoke a sense of nostalgia among subordinates for the previous leadership and its associated practices (Spillane et al., 2015). Followers accustomed to participating in decision-making processes and taking initiatives under the former transformational leader might assume they can continue in the same manner with the new leader, even if such behaviors are not solicited (Mattar, 2020). The new principal's approach to transformational leadership can vary significantly due to organizational culture and climate, relationships with staff, receptivity to change, and their own experience and expertise (Dimmock & Yong Tan, 2013). While new leaders bring fresh perspectives and are often tasked with a mandate for change, they face the challenge of building trust and credibility among their staff. They must carefully balance respecting the established practices and introducing new strategies that align with their vision for the school's future, navigating the delicate transformation process with sensitivity and assertiveness (Shoho & Barnett, 2010). Such transitions' complexity requires substantial managerial skills and external support from change consultants (Fusarelli et al., 2018).

Impact of Leadership Transition on Entrepreneurial Teacher Leaders

Teacher leaders play an essential role at schools, bridging the gap between administration and classroom instruction (Bryant et al., 2018). Their responsibilities extend beyond teaching; they often include curriculum development, coaching peers, fostering professional development, and implementing school improvement initiatives (Lipscombe et al., 2023). Leaders are expected to influence school culture positively, advocate for effective teaching strategies, and support adopting innovative practices (Ho et al., 2024). Their roles are important in translating educational policies into actionable plans that enhance teaching quality and student learning outcomes (Nobile et al., 2024). By actively participating in decision-making processes and taking initiative, teacher leaders help shape the educational environment better to meet the needs of the students and the community (Bryant & Rao, 2019).

However, the transition of principals can pose significant challenges for teacher leaders. New leadership often brings changes in vision, priorities, and strategies that can disrupt established procedures and relationships (Grice, 2019). During such transitions, teacher leaders may face uncertainties regarding role expectations and shifts in school culture, affecting their ability to perform effectively (Fusarelli et al., 2018). Adapting to new leadership styles and expectations can be stressful, particularly if the incoming principal has different views on teacher autonomy and leadership. Additionally, the loss of a supportive principal who championed teacher leadership can lead to a decrease in morale and a sense of instability, affecting the overall effectiveness of teacher leaders (Thorpe & Bennett-Powell, 2014).

Indeed, this chapter proposes that a principal transition can be particularly impactful for entrepreneurial teacher leaders who thrive on innovation and driving change. These leaders require a supportive environment that values risk-taking and creative problem-solving (Ho et al., 2022). When a new principal arrives, the uncertainty about their stance on innovation can hinder the entrepreneurial activities of teacher leaders (Listiningrum et al., 2020). If the new principal is less supportive of entrepreneurial initiatives, these leaders may have fewer opportunities to experiment with new teaching methods or implement groundbreaking programs. Conversely, a principal who understands and appreciates the value of entrepreneurial leadership can further empower these teachers, enhancing their impact on the school's advancement (Zhu et al., 2023). Thus, it is imperative to investigate the dynamics of entrepreneurial teacher leaders' perceptions of this change and their commitment to maintaining their entrepreneurial initiatives.

METHODOLOGY

This study employs a single case study approach to explore the unique circumstances and outcomes associated with a leadership transition at a Hong Kong secondary school, focusing on its impact on entrepreneurial teacher leaders. This method is advantageous for deeply understanding the specific processes that influence the behaviors of entrepreneurial teacher leaders within a clearly defined system. It enables the researcher to capture the richness and complexity of real-life events that, while unique, represent many other schools undergoing similar transitions. Consequently, this approach offers valuable implications for practice in developing teacher leaders.

Sampling

This study employed a purposeful sampling technique, guided by clearly defined criteria, to select our subject for this study: (1) the entrepreneurial teacher leader needed to demonstrate significant entrepreneurial initiative, and (2) the leader had to have experienced a transition of principalship within the same school. Based on recommendations from education authorities, Ms. Ann, a Hong Kong secondary school teacher, was identified as a particularly compelling candidate.

Ms. Ann's case provides a rich context for examining the influence of leadership transitions on entrepreneurial teacher leaders. She was profoundly influenced and inspired by a transformational principal who played a pivotal role in her development as an educational innovator. Under this principal's mentorship, Ms. Ann spearheaded a transformative initiative within the school's science, technology, engineering, and mathematics (STEM) curriculum. Under the tutelage of the transformational principal, she was encouraged to dream big, setting inspirational goals that resonated with colleagues and the students. The principal's vision for a cutting-edge STEM program served as a beacon, inspiring the teacher leader to reflect the core value of their school's STEM education. As their students are from gross-root class, he challenged her to think critically and creatively to design the STEM curriculum that fit students' social backgrounds, leading to a rigorous and engaging curriculum. The principal also recognized her unique talents and provided tailored mentorship, fostering an environment where she could grow professionally. The principal was a model the teacher leader aspired to emulate in her practice.

In the past five years, she has fostered a groundbreaking collaboration with a university, developing a distinctive STEM program tailored to her school's needs. Her innovative approach garnered attention beyond the school walls, earning her invitations to speak at the Hong Kong Education Expo and to serve as a part-time lecturer at the university, where she could share her entrepreneurial journey in education. Recognized for the success of STEM curriculum, the teacher leader advanced to a formal leadership position. However, two years later, the school faced a pivotal moment when the guiding principal retired. A new transformational leader with an impressive record of success in other schools was appointed.

The new principal introduced a distinct set of developmental agendas that shifted the school's focus from STEM education to value education, reflecting the broader demands of society and the job market. This principle also exemplified transformational leadership, invigorating colleagues with a shared purpose toward moral and civic values education.

Data Collection

Table 7.1 outlines this study's two primary data collection methods: interviews and meeting observations. I interviewed Ms. Ann, her former principal, the new principal, and two of her colleagues to gather diverse perspectives and create a comprehensive view of the leadership dynamics.

TABLE 7.1 Description of Data Sources

Data Sources	Description	Number of interview/ Observations
Interview		
Principal O	Principal, who employed and inspired Ms Ann, had retired.	One interview
Principal N	New principal in the secondary school.	One interview
Ms Ann	The key participant (STEM education coordinator).	Two interviews
Colleagues A	Ms Ann's team member.	One interview
Colleagues B	Another subject coordinator, who had worked with Ms. Ann to develop the curriculum, had collaborated with her for over five years.	One interview
Observation		
The STEM education meeting	A meeting where Ms. Ann was in charge of collaborating with teachers from other subject areas.	Two meetings

Additionally, observing meetings provided more profound insights into the school's operational environment under Ms. Ann's leadership. It served as a means to triangulate the data obtained from the interviews.

Data Analysis

The data were analyzed through three concurrent processes: data reduction, data display, and conclusion drawing (Miles et al., 2018). Initial data management commenced concurrently with data collection, gathering, reviewing, and storing preliminary notes.

During the data reduction phase, coding was applied to select pertinent findings for inclusion in this article. This phase included conducting member checks on the transcripts, preliminary coding based on the interview transcripts, and meeting observations. Data were initially categorized deductively into four types of codes: descriptive, emotional, attitudes, and value codes. Descriptive coding involved summarizing the topics, organizing, and interpreting the temporal sequences of events and changes in behaviors of entrepreneurial teacher leaders. Emotional, attitude, and value codes were used to label events with keywords that reflect the participants' values, attitudes, and beliefs (Miles et al., 2018). This approach facilitated the provision of "thick descriptions" that elucidated the values underpinning teacher actions.

In the data display phase, the categorized data were visually organized into tables to facilitate analysis. This visual organization helped identify patterns and themes across the coded data, providing a structured way to interpret complex relationships and processes. To enhance the validity of the coding process, participants were invited to verify both descriptive and interpretative codes. Subsequently, the data were reorganized to construct themes from the findings. These themes were synthesized from patterned codes to illustrate distinct longitudinal transitions among teachers.

FINDINGS

This section outlines three major themes: emerging challenges, refining the leader's role, and acting as a tactful leader. It describes entrepreneurial leaders' strategies to translate a new principal's vision into concrete, actionable outcomes that align with the entrepreneurial leader's original direction.

Theme 1—Emerging Challenges

Three key challenges entrepreneurial leaders face following the arrival of a new principal are: Navigating Directional Dilemmas, addressing Resource Allocation Challenges, and Building Trust.

Navigating Directional Dilemmas
The new principal previously oversaw students' pastoral care, which led her to shift the school's focus from a primarily academic orientation to a values-based education approach. However, this new direction has created dilemmas. The incorporated management committee (IMC) oversees school operations and believes that STEM education currently defines the school's brand. They argue that the school should invest more effort in further developing this area.

"We need to appease the IMC members while also supporting our principal. The challenge is that they have conflicting directions." (Colleague A)

Ms. Ann has found that the directional dilemma has created a ripple effect on her role. Since the arrival of the new principal, she has been put in charge of value education. At the same time, she continues to lead both the STEM and value education teams. This multitasking has left her feeling overloaded and uncertain about her priorities.

Resource Allocation Challenges
The ripple effect of directional dilemmas is evident in allocating human and financial resources. Since STEM education is no longer the primary

focus of school development, the new principal has redirected funding away from STEM activities and reassigned most experienced leaders to other teams.

"I have no money to organize extracurricular activities for my students. He said everything is well-established already. However, more resources are needed for the new initiatives." (Ms Ann)

The loss of financial and human resources has consequently limited the further development of STEM education.

Building Trust

Ms. Ann had a close relationship with the former principal, which allowed her to enter the principal's office without prior notification to discuss various issues. However, she has continued this practice with the new principal, which has caused discomfort.

"She always suddenly shows up in my office and asks permission to discuss various issues. It's quite unsettling that anyone can enter the principal's office whenever they want. I feel a bit insecure." (Principal N)

Ms. Ann finds the new principal's communication practices different from those of the previous principal, leading to feelings of disrespect. This mismatch in communication styles has made it difficult for them to find a comfort zone for sharing views, thereby hindering the development of a trustworthy relationship necessary for discussing issues effectively.

Theme 2—Refining the Leader's Role

The discomfort of working with the principals and the challenges of maintaining STEM education have prompted the entrepreneurial leader to reevaluate her role at the school. Overwhelmed with the workload, she realized that she needed to transition from being an executor to acting more as a coach.

Fostering Pipeline Leaders

Driven by frustration, Ms. Ann reflected on her experiences with the former principal, who demonstrated effective team assembly and the formation of a supportive team culture. These memories reminded her that she could no longer manage every task or make every decision as a senior leader responsible for two teams. She decided to train the next generation of leaders in this field to ensure the continuity of STEM education.

"Half of my team members are experienced colleagues, and half are new. ... I notice they are helpful but sometimes lose sight of our core mission. It's my responsibility to reignite their focus and empower them." (Ms. Ann)

She believes that her role has evolved from a doer to a coach who imparts practical knowledge to newer colleagues. This shift is not just about redistributing workload; it is about mentoring them to understand their tasks' 'how' and 'why'. She is committed to passing the torch to the next generation and grooming them to become leaders.

Synergizing Vision and Duty

Caught in the dilemma between the directions set by the IMC and the Principal, Ms. Ann felt a sense of urgency to address the issue of overload—a problem she realized was also affecting her team members. As a leader, she recognized her responsibility to ensure the effectiveness of both STEM and value education initiatives while managing multitasking challenges.

"Honestly, my interests lie in STEM and fostering students' values. Both are important to me. I see the need to ensure synergy between these initiatives, not just for my own benefit but for my colleagues. They need to see the connection between them." (Ms. Ann)

She attempted to reconceptualize the common features of both initiatives and listed all the tasks her team was working on. Through this process, she realized that their efforts were duplicating. Recognizing the need to transform these two school-level initiatives into a more coherent single team-level initiative, she began planning strategies to streamline their activities. Through this process, she recognized the need to refine her leadership role, embracing the responsibility of guiding and mentoring her team members toward a more unified and effective approach.

Theme 3—Acting as Tactful Leader

Since Ms. Ann recognized that the change in leadership led to dynamic shifts in school initiatives, resource allocation, and her role, she developed three tactful strategies. These strategies are designed to ensure STEM education's survival and address all their challenges.

Sounding Out the Principal's Expectations

Understanding the importance of garnering support from the principal, Ms. Ann strategically approached the principal on multiple occasions to ensure the legitimacy of both the STEM and Value education initiatives.

> She has discussed with me several times to understand my perspective on STEM and Value education. I noticed she had a general idea about them, which I clarified. This helped her grasp my expectations and the scope of these initiatives. Principal N.

Ms. Ann learned how to tactfully communicate with the principal to understand the primary goals and convey her interpretations. This approach was crucial not only to align the direction of both initiatives with the school's overall direction but also to secure the principal's endorsement of her suggestions.

Maximizing Informal Authority

Ms. Ann recognized the high autonomy the principal granted teachers in delivering STEM and value education, along with clear project direction and financial support primarily for value education. Seizing this opportunity, Ms. Ann sought to enhance the STEM education program.

"She approached a technology company to partner with us. Their mentoring scheme for students enriches our program and helps distribute our workload." (Colleague B)

"We secured a donation from a foundation, allowing us to hire an additional teaching assistant for our team." (Colleague A)

Understanding her formal authority to lead, Ms. Ann also utilized her network to expand her informal influence, thereby gaining additional resources. All resources obtained were integrated into the team's collective assets.

Ms. Ann merged the STEM and value education initiatives to maximize synergy and streamline efforts. This strategic consolidation was part of her broader vision to refine her leadership role and enhance team collaboration. Consequently, she organized an informal strategy session for both teams to collaborate on designing and implementing a unified initiative.

"My strategy is to use informal collaboration to merge these two initiatives effectively. This enables us to share resources and manpower, achieving more with less—essentially, hitting two birds with one stone." (Ms. Ann)

Through this informal authority, Ms. Ann strategically synergized resources, significantly reducing her colleagues' workloads. This approach alleviated pressure on individual team members and enhanced the overall effectiveness and innovation of the combined initiatives.

Pipelining Through Mentoring

To cultivate a pipeline of future leaders within her team, Ms. Ann shared her vision with experienced team members, prompting the creation of one-on-one mentoring relationships between seasoned and new team members.

"They act as both coaches and friends. Together, they design, deliver, and evaluate tasks." (Ms. Ann)

This mentoring strategy ensures that mentors guide mentees through every process, sharing insights and stories behind each task. The goal is to preserve the operational aspects and the spirit of their STEM education initiative, fostering strong trust among colleagues.

However, Ms. Ann recognized that new members often have their perspectives on their roles. Therefore, she tactfully provided two to three task options for each mentoring pair to choose from in delivering the STEM education. These options were carefully selected to fall within an acceptable scope, allowing teachers autonomy while ensuring alignment with the team's goals.

As a result, a new integrated STEM-value education program was established. Ms. Ann assumed the roles of coach and key decision-maker. This approach facilitated the growth of new leaders and established new working norms within and across the teams, enhancing collaboration and innovation in their educational strategies.

DISCUSSION

This study aims to illuminate the strategies used to mitigate the impacts of principal transitions on existing initiatives. The findings provide a detailed examination of how an entrepreneurial leader, such as Ms. Ann, refined her role to promote the sustainability and continuous improvement of STEM education initiatives during such transitions. The study highlights insightful strategies for leaders to consider when addressing the challenges posed by leadership changes. These strategies are designed to ensure that the momentum of critical educational programs is maintained and that these programs are sustained and enhanced under new leadership.

Unexpected Burden from Concurrent Initiatives

The findings indicate that the simultaneous pursuit of the IMC's focus on STEM education alongside the new principal's values-based education initiative has significantly increased the workload for entrepreneurial leaders like Ms. Ann. This dual-direction approach has created an intricate environment where resources are overstretched, leading to burnout and inefficiencies. Ms. Ann's experiences underscore the challenges of managing conflicting priorities within the school, emphasizing the critical need for strategic alignment and prioritization. Leaders must skillfully navigate these challenges to prevent overburdening their teams. The increased workload strains leaders and trickles down, adversely affecting team morale and productivity. This situation highlights the necessity for clear and unified organizational goals to maintain operational effectiveness.

Imitating Leadership Practices

The study also reveals that Ms. Ann and her peers often emulate the leadership practices of the former principal, reflecting a form of leadership learning and adaptation. This mimicry is based on their positive experiences and the past effectiveness of those strategies. While imitation is a valuable learning mechanism, it may inhibit innovation and adaptation to new leadership styles. The reliance on established leadership practices suggests a preference for familiarity, which may not align with the new principal's vision, potentially causing conflicts and resistance to change. This observation aligns with the literature on leadership transition, highlighting the importance of leaders adapting and evolving rather than solely relying on historical methods.

Restoring Team Culture

A crucial aspect of addressing these challenges is the restoration and reinforcement of a cohesive team culture. Ms. Ann's efforts to foster a supportive and collaborative environment are vital in mitigating the impacts of increased workload and leadership transition. By mentoring and empowering team members, she aims to rebuild trust and foster unity within the team. This strategy tackles immediate operational challenges and lays the groundwork for long-term organizational resilience. The significance of a robust team culture is well-documented in leadership literature, underscoring its role in boosting team performance, satisfaction, and overall success. Ms. Ann's proactive approach to restoring and strengthening the team culture is a strategic measure to ensure the sustainability of STEM and values-based education initiatives.

PRACTICAL IMPLICATIONS

Based on the findings regarding how entrepreneurial leaders handle transitions in principal leadership, here are the key practical implications:

- Leadership Transitions: New leaders should prioritize aligning their vision with that of key stakeholders. This alignment minimizes directional dilemmas and conflicts over resource allocation, ensuring a smoother transition.
- Resource Management: Effective resource management is crucial. Leaders must balance new initiatives' demands with existing programs' needs to prevent disenfranchising established teams.
- Trust and Communication: Building trust through adaptive communication strategies is essential for successfully navigating leadership transitions. Transparent and flexible communication can bridge gaps between old and new leadership practices.
- Leadership Development: Developing future leaders through mentorship and coaching is vital for the sustainability and resilience of educational programs. This approach ensures a continuous pipeline of capable leaders ready for future challenges.
- Leadership Flexibility and Adaptability: Team leaders must demonstrate high flexibility and adaptability during transitions. Adjusting to new dynamics and challenges is key to maintaining team coherence and effectiveness.

These implications offer actionable strategies for leaders undergoing transitions, aiming to enhance leadership effectiveness and organizational stability.

CONCLUSION

The case of Ms. Ann provides a vivid illustration of the challenges entrepreneurial leaders face during a principal transition. With the new principal shifting the focus from a predominantly academic orientation to a values-based education approach, Ms. Ann navigated complex directional dilemmas. The IMC's insistence on maintaining a strong STEM education program further compounded her challenges. This dual-directional mandate increased workload, resource allocation conflicts, and trust-building issues. Ms. Ann's adaptive leadership strategies, including fostering a pipeline of future leaders, synergizing vision and duties, and leveraging informal authority, highlight the critical role of flexibility and strategic alignment in managing such transitions. Her efforts to restore and reinforce team culture demonstrate the importance of cohesive and supportive environments in organizational change.

CASE STUDY

Transition at XYZ School—Balancing Tradition and Innovation

In this case study, the principal of XYZ School retires after a decade of emphasizing traditional academic excellence. The new principal, Dr. Smith, introduces a progressive education model focusing on holistic student development, including emotional intelligence and social skills. Teachers and staff, who have long been accustomed to the traditional model, face similar challenges of directional dilemmas, resource allocation conflicts, and trust-building issues. The case explores how entrepreneurial leaders within the school navigate these changes, balance tradition with innovation, and develop new strategies to align with Dr. Smith's vision while maintaining the school's academic standards.

REFLECTIONS ON THE CASE

- How can leaders effectively balance the demands of maintaining established tradition while integrating new initiatives introduced by a new principal?

- What strategies can leaders employ to build trust and foster effective communication with new principals who have different leadership styles and visions?
- In what ways can leaders use their informal authority and networks to secure additional resources and support for their initiatives during periods of organizational transition?

REFERENCES

Bass, B. M. (1985). *Leadership and performance beyond expectations.* Free Press.
Bass, B. M., & Riggio, R. E. (2006). *Transformational leadership.* Lawrene Erlbaum Associates, Inc..
Berkovich, I. (2016). School leaders and transformational leadership theory: Time to part ways? *Journal of Educational Administration, 54*(5), 609–622.
Bryant, D. A., Ko, J., & Walker, A. (2018). How do school principals in Hong Kong shape policy? *Leadership and Policy in Schools, 17*(3), 345–359. https://doi.org/10.1080/15700763.2018.1496340
Bryant, D. A., & Rao, C. (2019). Teachers as reform leaders in Chinese schools. *International Journal of Educational Management, 33*(4), 663–677.
Chand, V. S., & Amin-Choudhury, G. (2006). Teachers and socio-educational entrepreneurship: Competence as a consequence. *The Journal of Entrepreneurship, 15*(2), 97–114.
Davis, J. (2023). *How to become an entrepreneurial teacher: Being innovative, leading change.* Routledge.
Dimmock, C., & Yong Tan, C. (2013). Educational leadership in Singapore: Tight coupling, sustainability, scalability, and succession. *Journal of Educational Administration, 51*(3), 320–340.
Engelen, A., Gupta, V., Strenger, L., & Brettel, M. (2015). Entrepreneurial orientation, firm performance, and the moderating role of transformational leadership behaviors. *Journal of Management, 41*(4), 1069–1097.
Eyal, O., & Kark, R. (2004). How do transformational leaders transform organizations? A study of the relationship between leadership and entrepreneurship. *Leadership and Policy in Schools, 3*(3), 211–235.
Fitzgerald, S., & Schutte, N. (2010). Increasing transformational leadership through enhancing self-efficacy. *Journal of Management Development, 29*(5), 495–505.
Fontana, A., & Musa, S. (2017). The impact of entrepreneurial leadership on innovation management and its measurement validation. *International Journal of Innovation Science, 9*(1), 2–19.
Fullan, M. (2023). *The principal 2.0: Three keys to maximizing impact* (2nd ed.). Wiley-Blackwell.
Fusarelli, B. C., Fusarelli, L. D., & Riddick, F. (2018). Planning for the future: Leadership development and succession planning in education. *Journal of Research on Leadership Education, 13*(3), 286–313.
Grice, C. (2019). Distributed pedagogical leadership for the implementation of mandated curriculum change. *Leading and Managing, 25*(1), 56–71.

Hanson, J. (2017). Exploring relationships between K–12 music educators' demographics, perceptions of intrapreneuring, and motivation at work. *Journal of Research in Music Education, 65*(3), 309–327.

Ho, C. S. M., Bryant, D. A., & Jiafang, L. (2022). Nurturing teachers' entrepreneurial behavior in schools: Roles and responsibilities for school principals. *Leadership and Policy in Schools,* 1–17.

Ho, C. S. M., Bryant, D. A., & Walker, A. D. (2023a). Capturing interactions between middle leaders and teacher entrepreneurial behaviour: An examination through a person-environment fit model. *School Leadership & Management, 42*(5), 498–519.

Ho, C. S. M., Lee, T. T.-l., & Lu, J. (2023b). Enhancing school appeal: How experiential marketing influences perceived school attractiveness in the urban context. *Education and Urban Society.* https://doi.org/10.1177/00131245231205261

Ho, C. S. M., Lee, T. C. L., & Lu, J. (2024). Enhancing school appeal: How experiential marketing influences perceived school attractiveness in the urban context. *Education and Urban Society, 56*(6), 703–727. https://doi.org/10.1177/00131245231205261

Ho, C. S. M., Lu, J., & Bryant, D. A. (2020). The impact of teacher entrepreneurial behaviour: A timely investigation of an emerging phenomenon. *Journal of Educational Administration, 58*(6), 697–712.

Ho, C. S. M., Lu, J., & Bryant, D. A. (2021). Understanding teacher entrepreneurial behavior in schools: Conceptualization and empirical investigation. *Journal of Educational Change,* 1–30.

Jensen, S. M., & Luthans, F. (2006). Entrepreneurs as authentic leaders: Impact on employees' attitudes. *Leadership and Organization Development Journal, 27,* 646–666.

Joensuu-Salo, S., Peltonen, K., Hämäläinen, M., Oikkonen, E., & Raappana, A. (2021). Entrepreneurial teachers do make a difference–Or do they? *Industry and Higher Education, 35*(4), 536–546.

Jolanta, N. (2013). The expression of a principal's transformational leadership during the organizational change process: A case study of Lithuanian gêneral education schools. *Problems of Education in the 21st Century, 51,* 70–82.

Kılınç, A. Ç., Polatcan, M., Savaş, G., & Er, E. (2024). How transformational leadership influences teachers' commitment and innovative practices: Understanding the moderating role of trust in principal. *Educational Management Administration & Leadership, 52*(2), 455–474.

Kotter, J. (2012). *The heart of change.* Harvard Business School Press.

Kroth, M., & Boverie, P. (2009). Using the discovering model to facilitate transformational learning and career development. *Journal of Adult Education, 38*(1), 43–47.

Leitch, C. M., & Volery, T. (2017). Entrepreneurial leadership: Insights and directions. *International Small Business Journal, 35*(2), 147–156.

Leithwood, K. (2001). School leadership in the context of accountability policies. International. *Journal of Leadership in Education, 4*(3), 217–235.

Leithwood, K., Jantzi, D., & Steinbach, R. (2021). Leadership and other conditions which foster organizational learning in schools. In K. A. Leithwood & K. S. Louis (Eds.), *Organizational learning in schools* (pp. 67–90). Taylor & Francis.

Li, L., & Liu, Y. (2022). An integrated model of principal transformational leadership and teacher leadership that is related to teacher self-efficacy and student academic performance. *Asia Pacific Journal of Education, 42*(4), 661–678.

Lipscombe, K., Tindall-Ford, S., & Lamanna, J. (2023). School middle leadership: A systematic review. *Educational Management Administration & Leadership, 51*(2), 270–288.

Listiningrum, H. D., Wisetsri, W., & Boussanlegue, T. C. H. A. B. L. E. (2020). Principal's entrepreneurship competence in improving teacher's entrepreneurial skill in high schools. *Journal of Social Work and Science Education, 1*(1), 87–95.

Lovett, L. (2023). Teacher leadership and teachers' learning: Actualizing the connection from day one. *Professional Development in Education, 49*(6), 1010–1021. https://doi.org/10.1080/19415257.2023.2235583

Martin, A. M., Abd-El-Khalick, F., Mustari, E., & Price, R. (2018). Effectual reasoning and innovation among entrepreneurial science teacher leaders: A correlational study. *Research in Science Education, 48*, 1297–1319.

Mattar, D. M. (2020). The culmination stage of leadership succession. *Journal of Organizational Change Management, 33*(7), 1355–1373.

Miles, M. B., Huberman, A. M., & Saldaña, J. (2018). *Qualitative data analysis: A methods sourcebook*. Sage.

Nobile, J. D., Lipscombe, K., Tindall-Ford, S., & Grice, C. (2024). Investigating the roles of middle leaders in New South Wales public schools: Factor analyses of the Middle Leadership Roles Questionnaire. *Educational Management Administration & Leadership*. https://doi.org/10.1177/17411432241231871

Shoho, A. R., & Barnett, B. G. (2010). The realities of new principals: Challenges, joys, and sorrows. *Journal of School Leadership, 20*(5), 561–596.

Spillane, J. P., Harris, A., Jones, M., & Mertz, K. (2015). Opportunities and challenges for taking a distributed perspective: Novice school principals' emerging sense of their new position. *British Educational Research Journal, 41*(6), 1068–1085.

Thorpe, A., & Bennett-Powell, G. (2014). The perceptions of secondary school middle leaders regarding their needs following a middle leadership development programme. *Management in Education, 28*(2), 52–57.

Van Dam, K., Schipper, M., & Runhaar, P. (2010). Developing a competency-based framework for teachers' entrepreneurial behaviour. *Teaching and Teacher Education, 26*(4), 965–971.

Walker, A., & Riordan, G. (2010). Leading collective capacity in culturally diverse schools. *School Leadership and Management, 30*(1), 51–63.

Zappe, S. E., Cutler, S., & Litzinger, T. A. (2021, July). Work in progress: Impact of the Entrepreneurial Mindset for Innovative Teaching (EMIT) Academy. American Society for Engineer Education (ASEE). Virtual Annual Conference Content Access.

Zhao, G., Li, G., Jiang, Y., Guo, L., Huang, Y., & Huang, Z. (2022). Teacher entrepreneurship, co-creation strategy, and medical student entrepreneurship for sustainability: Evidence from China. *Sustainability, 14*(19), 12711.

Zhu, R., Liu, Z., Zhao, G., Huang, Z., & Yu, Q. (2023). Exploring the mediating role of teacher entrepreneurial behaviors in the relationship between institutional management and teacher entrepreneurship competency. *International Journal of Management Education, 21*, 100794. https://doi.org/10.1016/j.ijme.2023.100794

CHAPTER 8

TRANSFORMING SCHOOLS THROUGH REFLECTIVE DIALOGUE

Rachel D. Solis
Educational Coach, USA

ABSTRACT

In Chapter 8, Rachel Solis asserts that reflective dialogue facilitated effectively by educational leaders can transform perspectives and practices to improve schools. While reflection supports us to understand where we are and where we want to be, dialogue allows us to deprivatize beliefs and collectively work to actualize change. Leadership for school change through reflective dialogue entails fostering "deep conversations" centered around educational beliefs and the relationship between those beliefs and the school's day-to-day practices. Reflective dialogue, above all, challenges individual and institutional assumptions, explores diverse perspectives, fosters critical thinking, and leads to informed and intentional decision-making that enhances teaching and outcomes for students. Dr. Solis, an educational coach and consultant working with classroom teachers, departmental teams, and school leaders to foster reflective dialogue, shares examples and insights from the literature and practice to demonstrate the power of reflective dialogue to empower and encourage shared leadership and align the connection between the specifics of school practices and student learning.

Keywords: Leading school change; critical thinking in education; reflective dialogue; instructional coaching; educational coaching; school practices

> *Prefocus Guiding Questions*
>
> - What is the relationship between reflective dialogue and transformative learning?
> - If you were to visit a school with which you are unfamiliar, what indicators would you look for to determine whether the school was implementing reflective dialogue?
> - What conditions and methods for reflective dialogue would you like to see implemented or improved in a school you are familiar with?

INTRODUCTION

Affecting significant change in schools requires an understanding of where we are and envisioning where we want to be, and reflection is a key element to achieving that understanding. Reflection supports us as we consider the school's culture and all that comprises that culture, needed changes, and avenues to improvement. Refection alone, however, is not enough to propel an organization forward. Reflection paired with dialogue deprivatizes beliefs and can move a school toward collective efforts to actualize school change. Reflective dialogue facilitated effectively by educational leaders can transform perspectives and practices to improve schools.

Leadership for school improvement through reflective dialogue entails fostering "deep conversations" (Nelson et al., 2010) on educational beliefs and the relationship between those beliefs and the school's day-to-day practices. According to Nelson and associates (2010), the impact of dialogue among educators in schools "is expanded or limited by the nature of conversations" (p. 175) and, as such, transformative dialogue requires a shift from sharing to inquiry, from superficial to deep discourse, and from congenial to collegial conversation. Reflective dialogue that probes deeply can challenge individual and institutional assumptions, explore diverse perspectives, foster critical thinking, and lead to informed and intentional decision-making that enhances teaching and learning. Transformation does not happen without changing beliefs, and it is reflective dialogue in the form of "robust discourse" that "leads to teachers locating their own understandings and beliefs within a wider conversation, ensuring that beliefs are not viewed as inevitable but chosen" (Wallen & Tormey, 2019, p. 138).

This chapter focuses on reflective dialogue as a tool for changing perspectives, practices, and schools. The three main areas to be addressed are (a) the relationship between reflective dialogue and transformative learning, (b) conditions necessary for educators to engage in reflective dialogue, including common challenges for school leaders, and (c) methods for educational leaders to facilitate reflective dialogue and the impact of that dialogue on teaching and learning. Insights and examples from the literature and practice will demonstrate how "the experience [of reflective dialogue] can be transformational as teachers are able to recognize and resolve cognitive dissonance, inspiring changes in behaviors and beliefs" (Glickman et al., 2024, p. 96).

LITERATURE REVIEW

Reflective Dialogue and Transformative Learning

Reflective dialogue is discussed in various ways in the literature on educational leadership, professional development, and practitioner inquiry. To enhance teaching and learning through reflective dialogue, authors in these disciplines describe:

- "constructive conversations": identifying and reflecting on personal beliefs and dispositions that impact teaching, especially in terms of culture, to better understand students (Wilcoxen et al., 2022)
- "productive dialogue": positioning challenges as sources of growth, considering the motivations behind actions, and moving toward new ways of responding to struggle (Stewart & Jansky, 2022)
- "open communication": sharing experiences and challenges to identify patterns, triggers, and successful solutions (Iraola et al., 2024)
- "deep discourse": discussing substantive issues, defining the problem, and generating solutions (Brantlinger et al., 2011)
- "critical reflection": identifying, questioning, and jointly reflecting on the reasons why we believe and behave in a certain way and the assumptions associated with those beliefs and behaviors (Nijhuis, 2021)
- "dialogic reflective inquiry": combining reflection and dialogue within each phase of recurring cycles of inquiry, including problem framing, gathering and analyzing data, planning and implementation, and assessment (Gordon, 2008)

The descriptions above share a critical common thread: reflective dialogue is not "merely working alongside another teacher" or engaging in "casual communication" (Iraola et al., 2024); rather, it is the exchanging of ideas, the examining of assumptions, and the collective sense-making (Wallen & Tormey, 2019) that supports an "evolution of pedagogy" (Iraola et al., 2024). It calls for intentional, purposeful thinking and conversation to analyze perspectives and to understand one's own beliefs and biases and how these impact one's decision-making. The ultimate goal of reflective dialogue is transformative learning, also referred to as "double-loop learning," that not only improves the way things are done, but "transforms the situation" (Brockbank et al., 2017).

According to Ben-Peretz and colleagues (2018), reflective dialogue is a joint effort "to address the issue at hand by engaging with different perspectives, enabling the deliberation to problematize assumptions that formerly seemed stable" (p. 306)—making the familiar unfamiliar! It is in these moments of increased awareness of how our beliefs manifest in practice that we may experience cognitive dissonance, at which time we are faced with the need to resolve the dissonance, ultimately in ways that improve teaching and learning. Absent such moments of felt difficulty, assumptions remain undiscovered and stable. On the other hand, "when we become increasingly attuned to our beliefs, decision making evolves, and teaching and learning improve as decisions become more informed and intentional" (Glickman et al., 2024, p. 100).

As opposed to top-down, compliance-driven transmissive learning, transformative learning experiences provide educators with "opportunities to reflect through dialogue to deepen their learning and apply it to practice" (Miller, 2024, p. 42). In a study on teachers' perceptions of agency, Wallen and Tormey (2019) found that as teachers participated in reflective dialogue, they began to more frequently express their own self-agency, "awakening the sense that they were activists with expert knowledge who held a responsibility to address the needs of [their] learners" (p. 138). Solis and Gordon (2020) discovered similar findings in a study of teachers engaged in a reflective inquiry process. Through ongoing reflective dialogue, the teachers began to accept ownership for changes they wished to see and moved toward becoming "agents of change" committed to continuously analyzing their beliefs and how those beliefs inform their practices. Reflective dialogue assisted teachers to examine their teaching platforms alongside their teaching behaviors, and all participants agreed that "it was important to take this conscious, though sometimes difficult, look at themselves" to provide "the discomfort needed to stimulate change" (p. 19).

Reflective dialogue—facilitated effectively by educational leaders, between leaders and teachers, and among teachers—can transform perspectives and practices to improve schools. But what conditions do teachers need in place to publicly examine their thinking and analyze their practices? And what are common challenges that school leaders face with implementing and facilitating reflective dialogue? The next section addresses these questions.

Conditions and Challenges

For teachers to experience transformative learning through reflective dialogue and take the risk inherent in such change efforts, certain organizational conditions need to be fostered, including a learning culture that embraces and embodies reflective dialogue, a safe and supportive environment for teacher learning, opportunities and time to engage in reflective dialogue, professional learning to cultivate requisite knowledge and skills, and shared leadership to develop dispositions for reflective dialogue. Each of these conditions can pose challenges for school leaders as they work to build organizational capacity to develop a culture of reflective dialogue for continuous school improvement.

Condition 1: A Learning Culture that Embraces and Embodies Reflective Dialogue

Across various perspectives of professional development for school change, Butler and Schnellert (2012) found two consistent themes: "(a) a fundamental commitment to improving outcomes for students, and (b) an emerging recognition that, to make a difference, change must be meaningfully situated and sustained at the classroom level" (p. 1206). These authors argue that professional development models that position teachers as central to the school improvement process foster meaningful change by "engaging teachers jointly in locally situated, inquiry-based, longitudinal, and critical examinations of practice" (p. 1206). Reflective dialogue, as described in the previous section, is a key element in such inquiry-based, critical examinations of practice, as it supports teachers' learning and leads to changes in their dispositions and practices.

Reflective dialogue calls for "the transformation of teaching into community property by making it visible and valuable by peer review" (Ben-Peretz et al., 2018, p. 304). Iraola and associates (2024) describe this type of learning community as being in "social synchrony," with high levels of professional engagement and interpersonal connections throughout the organization. A learning culture that embraces and embodies reflective dialogue schoolwide does not do so by employing a top-down, hierarchical leadership approach; instead, it empowers the collective! By empowering everyone in the organization, school leaders "make certain that everyone has easy access to the organization's expertise—its collective brain...a tightly woven web of informed, coordinated effort" (Hattie & Smith, 2021, p. 18). In empowering learning communities, teachers' self-efficacy and their ability and motivation to implement reform-oriented practices such as reflective dialogue increase as they are included in decision making and involved in the processes of professional development planning, implementation, and evaluation (Podolsky et al., 2019; Svendsen, 2020). A learning community of teachers actively working to examine their beliefs and develop their teaching skills creates "a network of knowledge and support for all members of the school community" (Glickman et al., 2024).

A school with a professional learning culture that embraces and embodies reflective dialogue schoolwide has:

- developed "a broad set of principles" to direct and evaluate the change process (Glickman et al., 2024, p. 392)
- committed to a schoolwide focus on reflective dialogue and the continuous improvement of teaching and learning through reflective dialogue (Messiou & Ainscow, 2020; Solis & Gordon, 2019)
- adopted an "informed agency approach" to professional development that empowers teachers to "seek the potential expert within" (Wallen & Tormey, 2019, p. 130)
- fostered "hospitable niches in which new practices can take root, grow and be sustainable over the longer term" (Wilkinson, 2014, p. 29)
- focused more on the conditions under which reflective dialogue occurs and the effects of that dialogue, rather than focusing mainly on the activities themselves (Svendsen, 2020, p. 115)

Reflective dialogue and methods for facilitating reflective dialogue are complex processes that require a long-term commitment by school leaders. The vision is a collaborative, inquiry-based, professional learning culture with common values and goals regarding reflective dialogue, structures and resources to support the process, and systems to monitor implementation and outcomes. Over time, "rich collaboration" (Butler & Schnellert, 2012) can become the norm across the campus.

Condition 2: A Safe and Supportive Environment For Teacher Learning
When we expose our thinking and practice to others, we make ourselves vulnerable (Colton et al., 2015; Twyford et al., 2017). Twyford et al. (2017) explain that "risk and uncertainty are inherent in learning, and can therefore create discomfort and apparent reluctance to engage as new learning replaces previously comfortable practices" (p. 97). While vulnerability is an essential aspect for professional learning, it "can impede participation and reflection unless it is accompanied by a sense of relational trust" (Miller, 2024). With trust, feedback is more easily given and received, and more effective (Bergmark, 2023; Brantlinger et al., 2011). Reflective dialogue necessitates mutual trust to "open up dialogic spaces" for sharing knowledge and negotiating meaning (Matre & Solheim, 2016).

Teachers engaging in inquiry into their practices are more willing to try new ideas and take risks, and they make greater gains in their teaching effectiveness, provided they belong to a collegial and supportive professional community (Jarvis et al., 2021; Podolsky et al., 2019; Svendsen, 2020) where they "feel comfortable expressing their opinions and actively participating in dialogue and critical reflection" (Rusov, 2023, p. 73). In a study of professional learning communities, Nijhuis (2021) found that "emotional safety" was the condition that emerged most strongly for reflective dialogue. Establishing trust between school leaders and teachers and among teachers allows teachers to analyze their practices in relation to their beliefs, and to recognize cognitive dissonance (Solis & Gordon, 2020). School leaders can find a balance between fostering too much or too little cognitive dissonance (both inhibit risk taking and learning!) by acknowledging perceived risk, sharing in the vulnerability of learning and change, and building trust (Brockbank et al., 2017; Miller, 2024; Wilcoxen et al., 2022). Twyford and associates (2017) encourage school leaders to remember that, in efforts to improve outcomes for students, teachers are also learners.

Acknowledging and addressing teacher wellbeing as an essential component of professional development programs is vital to school improvement (Glickman & Burns, 2020; Glickman et al., 2024). Muhonen and associates (2024) found that teachers who experience high levels of stress tend to have lower quality interactions with their students; whereas, a safe and supportive professional learning environment can "enhance the quality of classroom dialogue and further student learning" (p. 552). Teachers' perceptions of risk and their level of risk taking are impacted by perceived quality of the learning environment and the social relationships within that environment (Twyford et al., 2017).

Condition 3: Opportunities and Time to Engage in Reflective Dialogue

The most cited obstacle in the literature to ensuring that teachers have opportunities and sufficient time to engage thoroughly in reflective dialogue is time itself (Butler & Schnellert, 2012; Messiou & Ainscow, 2020; Solis & Gordon, 2019; Stewart & Jansky, 2022). Some scholars address this issue by arguing that a school's professional development policies should include teacher teams and professional teacher conversations as policy (Ronfeldt et al., 2015; van Kruiningen, 2013). This line of thinking aligns with the first condition for supporting teachers to engage in reflective dialogue: establishing a learning culture that embraces and embodies reflective dialogue. School leaders can "activate and scale collaborative expertise by orchestrating opportunities for teachers and school leaders to come together, reflect, and act on their reflection" (Hattie & Smith, 2021, p. 18). Embedding opportunities for reflective dialogue into the teachers' work day must be a priority. Reflective dialogue assists in making the work work for all students! The importance of "nurturing these processes with coordinated strategies and structures, along with the necessary time for a reflective process" (Iraola et al., 2024, p. 6) cannot be overstated. When a school's professional learning culture is not aligned with reflective dialogue, opportunities and time for such dialogue are hard to come by, and unsustainable over time.

Ronfeldt and colleagues (2015) studied instructional teams and the level and quality of collaboration that existed in those teams, as well as the relationship of that collaboration to student achievement. They found what we might expect: higher quality and levels of collaboration are associated with gains in teacher improvement and student achievement. High-quality collaboration provides the "space" needed for teachers to examine and strengthen their instruction, resulting in improved learning outcomes for students (Solis & Gordon, 2019). How does this work? Teachers engaged in reflective dialogue "collaborate in collecting evidence to stimulate new thinking and practices" (Messiou & Ainscow, 2020, p. 14). Messiou and Ainscow (2020) discuss the power of "creating interruptions" to challenge a teacher's thinking and encourage experimentation with new ideas for practice. Examples of interruptions—and potential vehicles for reflective dialogue—include collegial support groups, pre- and post-observation conferences with a critical friend, inquiry partnerships, planning and reviewing lessons with colleagues, participating in school-based teams, and peer coaching (Butler & Schnellert, 2012; Messiou & Ainscow, 2020; Solis & Gordon, 2019; Solis & Gordon, 2020). Some of these examples and others, such as collaborative action research (CAR), will be discussed in more detail in the section Methods and Impacts.

Collaboration and reflection take time to develop (King & Kitchener, 2004; Wilcoxen et al., 2022), and when school leaders facilitate opportunities for reflective dialogue, it supports the process of experimentation and continues to build "educators' capacity to routinely question their practice and teaching" (Miller, 2024, p. 35). Embedding time for teachers to think about and discuss context-specific "problems" they encounter in their daily work assists teachers to define the problems, recognize cognitive dissonance, achieve new understandings, and make informed changes to their practices.

Condition 4: Professional Learning to Cultivate Requisite Knowledge and Skills

Moving a school's learning environment "beyond mere transmission to a dynamic collaboration that fosters reflection, development, and excellence" is a crucial role of the school leader (Iraola et al., 2024), and it necessitates professional learning to cultivate requisite knowledge and skills for engaging in reflective dialogue (Iraola et al., 2024; Rusov, 2023; Wilkinson, 2014). Furthermore, to support teachers to "negotiate teaching tensions in authentic, reciprocal, and context-informed ways" (Alford & Jensen, 2021), teachers must be recognized and supported as individual learners with unique needs (Glickman et al., 2024; Solis & Gordon, 2020).

Teachers' *knowledge* and understanding of certain aspects of reflective dialogue is critical to the process of fostering productive collaboration and dialogue among teachers. It is important for teachers to know and understand that:

- Being attuned to the community context of the school supports teachers to teach in ways that meet the needs of all students (Wilcoxen et al., 2022).
- Challenging and respectful conversations promote growth in understanding and practices (Miller, 2024).
- Personal beliefs and dispositions impact teaching, and understanding this is essential for developing culturally relevant practices (Nelson et al., 2010; Wilcoxen et al., 2022).
- Collaboration focused on (a) student data and instructional responses, and (b) curricular and instructional decision making is most likely to promote gains in student learning and achievement (Ronfeldt et al., 2015).

Butler and Schnellert (2012) developed criteria for judging the depth and quality of collaborative relationships, ranging in five levels from "no collaboration" to "iterative shared inquiry into practice and teacher learning" (p. 1218). In this highest level of collaborative relationships, Butler and Schnellert's criteria include setting shared goals for students; setting and sharing goals for one's own professional learning; ongoing co-planning with sustained conversation about goals as related to practices; sharing and critiquing each other's classroom examples; ongoing co-reflection, problem-solving, and adaptation of approaches; longitudinal collaborative work within an inquiry cycle; and a shared inquiry stance toward practice and learning goals.

In addition to requisite knowledge for reflective dialogue, there are also *skills* that aid in the process:

- communication skills
- reflective questioning skills
- classroom observation skills
- gathering and analyzing data
- giving and receiving feedback
- identifying beliefs and assumptions
- recognizing cognitive dissonance
- using artifacts and evidence to mediate dialogue

Nijhuis (2021) discusses four levels of reflective communication, with "restricted" as the lowest level and "interactive" as the highest level. In the interactive mode, teachers seek other perspectives, share feedback, inquire into the nature of the problem, identify alternative solutions, utilize external knowledge and information to inform decision making, and reflect on and evaluate progress.

As school leaders work to cultivate knowledge and skills for reflective dialogue, there are some common challenges they encounter: (a) teachers' hesitation to examine their practice with others (Brantlinger et al., 2011); (b) a "watering down" of the reflective dialogue approach to where it falls short of challenging assumptions and stimulating experimentation (Messiou & Ainscow, 2020); (c) a fear of "research" (Bergmark, 2023); (d) the need to scaffold support to combat "continued reliance" on a facilitator (Bergmark, 2023); (e) fostering authentic dialogue that does not feel "artificial" (Alford & Jensen, 2021; Nijhuis, 2021); (f) providing meaningful feedback in a non-intrusive way (Alford & Jensen, 2021); and (g) reconciling theory and practice, especially regarding policies that impact teacher autonomy (Stewart & Jansky, 2022).

One idea to address these challenges is to monitor implementation of reflective dialogue with a "levels of use" instrument where teachers occasionally rate their level of use based on (a) a start has been made, (b) partial implementation, and (c) fully in place (Messiou & Ainscow, 2020, p. 7). These periodic self-assessments could be a great topic for reflective dialogue!

Condition 5: Shared Leadership to Develop Dispositions For Reflective Dialogue

Engaging in reflective dialogue as a professional learning process also requires key dispositions to influence the way teachers think and act (Dunn, 2021). A "shared leadership" approach to school improvement supports the development of dispositions for reflective dialogue by embracing teachers as professionals rather than technicians (Svendsen, 2020) and building "professional capital" (Podolsky et al., 2019). School leaders enacting shared leadership facilitate the development of strong relationships to establish "rich engagements" (Butler & Schnellert, 2012). Moving away from a "reductive typology" of teaching, a shared leadership approach recognizes "the range of experiences, skills, and knowledge that teachers bring to their learning" (Svendsen, 2020, p. 118).

Dispositions that support teachers to bring their experiences, skills, and knowledge to the table for reflective dialogue include: (a) agency—belief in one's self and abilities, (b) autonomy—taking ownership for one's own learning and growth, (c) awareness—becoming aware of one's beliefs and practices, (d) an inquiry stance—curiosity and a systematic approach to learning and change, and (e) critical reflection—questioning one's own beliefs and practices. Hargreaves and O'Connor (2018) discuss the essential shift schools must make from professional collaboration to collaborative professionalism, the latter characterized by a "commitment to collective responsibility for all students' success" (p. 12). Dispositions for reflective dialogue support this shift, but it does necessitate a long-term view. Similar to cultivating knowledge and skills for reflective dialogue, it takes time to develop the dispositions and thoughtful effort to sustain them, again with an understanding that teachers are individual learners with unique professional learning needs (Glickman et al., 2024; Solis & Gordon, 2020).

Methods and Impacts

Reflective dialogue aims to explore diverse perspectives, foster critical thinking that challenges assumptions, and inform intentional decision making that enhances teaching and learning, and there are myriad ways for school leaders to create opportunities for reflective dialogue in their schools. This section provides a few examples of methods educational leaders have used to facilitate reflective dialogue and the impact of that dialogue on teaching and learning.

"Video Club"—A Community of Practice

Brantlinger and associates (2011) report on a group of teachers who created a "video club" to examine video excerpts of their teaching in preparation for National Board certification. These secondary mathematics teachers met 16 times over a five-month period to engage in reflective dialogue about mathematics discourse, specifically techniques for facilitating discourse in their classrooms, contextual factors that affect student discourse, and criteria for evaluating discourse. Findings indicate that the video club experience was instrumental in assisting teachers to evolve in their ability to give and receive feedback on teaching and learning, and to reflect on their own beliefs and practices. Viewing and discussing the videos as a group was "key to the development" of their reflections and the evolution of their dialogue from "surface-level feedback and descriptions of videotaped activity, to discussions of deep, problematic issues" (p. 27).

Through ongoing reflective dialogue, the teachers "developed a shared vision of productive mathematical discourse and a shared language for describing it" (p. 29). They evolved in their beliefs about mathematical discourse and changed their practices accordingly. For example, in group review of one teacher's classroom video excerpt, another member of the group expressed that not many of the teacher's questions were eliciting response from students. Subsequent group discussions focused on questioning techniques that might enhance student responses and the teacher's progress with implementation. This group of teachers was engaged in problem-defining, solution-generating dialogue, intentionally designed by the teachers themselves to expose their thinking and practices, and to support informed changes to enhance student learning. The video club meetings served as a vehicle for making teacher knowledge explicit.

Brantlinger and colleagues argue that video is an effective tool—or "artifact of practice"—for reflecting on one's teaching and aiding in professional development because it can "capture the richness of classroom interactions" while allowing extended time for reflection, multiple viewings, and feedback from other perspectives. Results from the study indicate that group analysis of video excerpts led to a co-constructed vision of "worthwhile" classroom discourse, a shared approach to facilitation of such discourse, and a shared repertoire of practices. Teachers' beliefs and practices regarding mathematical discourse evolved from "typical classroom discourse" to "open and flexible discourse" in which "teachers probe the reasoning behind students' ideas, elicit a range of responses from students, and encourage students to build on each other's thinking" (p. 8). According to Brantlinger and colleagues, the video club supported the development of a professional learning community through the development of a shared purpose, reflective dialogue about substantive aspects of teaching and learning, and the sharing of teachers' practices.

Integrating Multiple Professional Learning Frameworks

Solis and Gordon (2020) describe a study that integrated multiple formats for professional learning in a reflective inquiry process to examine the impact on teaching beliefs and behaviors. The formats used in the study included action research, a critical friend, reflective writing, a collegial support group, and clinical supervision.

The reflective inquiry process centered on *action research* as each participant selected a focus area and engaged in recurring cycles of data gathering, reflective dialogue, and action. The remaining learning formats supported the teachers' action research. The *critical friend* facilitated all aspects of the reflective inquiry process. Participants engaged in *reflective writing* when they wrote their educational platforms at the start of the study, and periodically throughout the study when they reflected on their platforms and teaching actions in a journal. During *collegial support group* meetings the teachers shared progress and feedback with each other. Cycles of *clinical supervision* (pre-observation conference, classroom observation, and post-observation conference) provided the teachers with data for their action research and for comparison of their teaching beliefs and behaviors.

Teachers reported that the opportunity to engage in professional dialogue with the critical friend and with colleagues in the collegial support group was the component of the study they most appreciated; however, findings also indicated that dialogue "fostered teacher learning only when it involved reflective questions and encouragement that supported self-reflection and inquiry rather than excuses and blame" (p. 20). Another finding from the study was that each teacher experienced cognitive dissonance through the integration of the professional learning formats and reflective inquiry, which led to efforts to change their teaching practices. One of the teachers whose focus was on assessment of student learning realized that her assessment actions were not aligning with her true beliefs about assessment, and that both her beliefs and actions had gradually been influenced by ongoing external pressures over the years. As the teacher reconnected with her true beliefs about assessment, "she was able to assess student learning in more authentic and diverse ways" (p. 17). While realizations like this took time to materialize, by "allowing others to help them clarify their beliefs, and to realize that their teaching behaviors had fallen short of those beliefs, the teachers felt a responsibility to resolve that dissonance" (p. 20).

"Wobble" Stories—An Oral Inquiry Process

Stewart and Jansky (2022) employed an oral inquiry process to support novice teachers "to bring challenges they encounter in their first years of teaching into productive dialogue" and to help them "explore and learn from the underlying sources of tension within those struggles" (p. 3). Stewart and Jansky refer to the challenges teachers face as "moments of wobble" and explain that challenges can become stimuli for growth when teachers have the time and space to consider the causes of a specific challenge and explore a range of perspectives regarding the challenge and possible responses.

To begin the oral inquiry process, a teacher who has volunteered to be the session leader reads their "wobble" story, a narrative composed prior to the session that details a challenging teaching moment from the year. Following the reading, the group can ask clarifying questions, being careful not to phrase questions as "veiled attempts" to suggest a particular action. Next, the group writes responses to three questions: What stood out in this narrative? What connections did you make to this narrative? What issues did you identify in this narrative? Group members take turns sharing their responses to each question while the session leader takes notes. The session concludes with the session leader sharing ideas that resonated with them.

According to Stewart and Jansky, the teacher participants in this study had two main struggles: reconciling theory and practice, and managing relationships with veteran teachers. Through the oral inquiry group discussions, the teachers were able to clarify these struggles. For example, one of the teachers realized that curriculum and pacing expectations set by his school were not compatible with learning goals set by the state. Other teachers in the group expressed similar concerns and described their experiences with this same struggle.

Though this process provided teachers with information regarding the issues presented in their narratives, Stewart and Jansky found that it did not "result in a deeper, intentional exploration of the less obvious *why* behind these tensions and emotions and *what* someone might do about them" (p. 7). They propose an additional step "to cultivate discussion that explores the nuances in the sources of tension and takes an introspective turn toward productive emotion and action" (p. 7). To this end, Stewart and Jansky advise that a professional development facilitator support deeper dialogue by crafting questions for reflection specific to issues raised during the discussion, and they share a few potential questions as examples: Where am I now and where do I want to go in relation to this issue? How might I close the gap between the two? Are my emotions causing me to discount another perspective? How might my visceral response be shaping my view of the challenge or the source of the challenge? Group members reflect on the questions, respond in writing, and then take turns sharing their responses.

This study highlights an important point about reflective dialogue: talking with other teachers does not guarantee that reflective dialogue will occur. The "nature of the conversations" (Nelson et al., 2010) is key to transformative learning.

Collaborative Action Research

In a study of CAR by Gordon and Solis (2018), teams of teachers—led by teacher leaders who had previously completed professional development training on the ins and outs of CAR—engaged in independent action research on schoolwide issues at their respective schools. Each team conducted a needs assessment, selected a focus area for the CAR, and designed an action plan. One of the teams focused on increasing cultural responsiveness at their school. Though their ultimate goal was to expand the CAR to the entire school the following year, the first year of the CAR focused only on the team and its members, their current understanding of culturally responsive teaching, and anticipated growth.

For the CAR project, the teacher leader led the group of six teachers through six sessions of group dialogue centered on articles about culturally responsive teaching that were shared with the group to read in preparation for each meeting. The articles focused on the following topics: (a) norms for meaningful conversations, (b) the myth of the culture of poverty, (c) cultural myths regarding a specific population of students at the school, (d) how school discipline practices discriminate against historically disadvantaged groups, and proposed alternative strategies, (e) a multi-step process for teacher reflection aimed at overcoming deficit thinking, and (f) critical teacher reflection and culturally relevant pedagogy.

Post-survey results revealed that the teachers had become more reflective about their practices and that their understanding of culturally responsive teaching had increased. Results also indicated that the teachers had realized their teaching could be more culturally responsive, and they committed to incorporating more culturally responsive teaching practices into their teaching. The action plan the CAR team created for the future called for "ongoing, consistent and structured professional development centered around the theme of caring for students" (Gordon & Solis, 2018, p. 13), and the plan included specific action items such as implementing restorative circles, increasing involvement in the community, and adjusting teaching practices to reach all students.

The teacher leader facilitated reflective dialogue during the group sessions by maintaining positive interpersonal relationships within the group, and by displaying "flexibility, creative problem solving, and perseverance" (Gordon & Solis, 2018, p. 20) throughout the CAR. The authors contend that these attributes were essential for navigating "the hills and valleys" of the CAR process.

PRACTICAL IMPLICATIONS

School leaders wanting to implement or improve the quality and level of reflective dialogue at their school might consider the following:

- Taking note of the conversations occurring throughout the school
- Visiting other schools to observe for indicators of reflective dialogue and talking with other school leaders about the structures and processes they have in place for reflective dialogue, as well as the challenges they encounter
- Discussing *reflective dialogue* with the faculty and asking teachers to self-assess their current "levels of use" (Messiou & Ainscow, 2020)
- Conducting a faculty survey, interviews, and small-group discussions to gather data on teachers' perceptions of the conditions for reflective dialogue at their school
- Assisting interested teachers to engage in practitioner inquiry to study the process of reflective dialogue and its impact and to share their findings

CONCLUSION

It requires more than a leap of faith to ensure that a leader's actions influence teachers' practice, resulting in equity and enhanced learning for all students. Reflective dialogue is a practical and profound tool for school leaders to take that leap with an intention to align the connection between the specifics of school practices and desired outcomes for students. Dialogue can either "promote innovative teaching strategies or perpetuate conservative pedagogical practice" (Iraola et al., 2024, p. 4), and reflective dialogue, by its very nature, moves us toward innovation, transforming beliefs and behaviors and improving schools.

CASE STUDY

A group of Valley View Middle School teachers has agreed to engage in peer coaching to improve teaching and learning in their classrooms. The group's plan is to meet on a regular basis throughout the year to view video clips of each other teaching and engage in dialogue after each viewing. In her second year at the school, the principal asked teachers to select a professional learning format to examine context-specific problems of practice, with one stipulation: the format must include an avenue for dialogue.

Six teachers are participating in the peer coaching group, and they teach a variety of grade levels from 6-8 and have a range of teaching experience from 1 to 25 years. Three of the teachers in the group have less than five years of teaching experience, and the other three have been at Valley View for over ten years, one in his 25th year at the school. Valley View is located in an urban area, one of several middle schools, and the community it serves is approximately 45% Hispanic, 45% White, and 8% Black, with a small Asian population, and economically diverse. The previous principal of Valley View for over 20 years focused on creating a "comfortable" school environment; professional dialogue was rare, and when it did occur, it was an isolated event and not connected to a school-wide improvement effort.

For each group meeting, the teachers have decided that a different member of the group will volunteer to record a 15-minute segment of their teaching prior to the meeting and then share their video clip with the group at the meeting. The teachers are interested in trying peer coaching with group dialogue and want the experience to be productive; however, they are concerned about the process, specifically about what to record and how to facilitate the dialogue. The group has asked the school leader for assistance in getting started.

REFLECTIONS ON THE CASE

- What principles of reflective dialogue might the principal assist the teachers in establishing for group discussion after viewing a teacher's video clip?
- Regarding interpersonal interactions and topics of conversation during the group meetings, what growth should the school leader watch for as the meetings proceed over time?
- What indicators would demonstrate that the group dialogue positively affected teaching and learning in the participating teachers' classrooms?

REFERENCES

Alford, K., & Jensen, A. (2021). Cultivating dialogic reflection to foster and sustain preservice teachers' professional identities. *Teaching/Writing: The Journal of Writing Teacher Education, 10*(1), 8.

Ben-Peretz, M., Gottlieb, E., & Gideon, I. (2018). Coaching between experts—opportunities for teachers' professional development. *Teacher Development, 22*(3), 303–313.

Bergmark, U. (2023). Teachers' professional learning when building a research-based education: Context-specific, collaborative and teacher-driven professional development. *Professional Development in Education, 49*(2), 210-224.

Brantlinger, A., Sherin, M. G., & Linsenmeier, K. A. (2011). Discussing discussion: A video club in the service of math teachers' National Board preparation. *Teachers and Teaching: Theory and Practice, 17*(1), 5–33.

Brockbank, A., McGill, I., & Beech, N. (2017). The nature and context of learning. In *Reflective learning in practice* (pp. 5–17). Routledge.

Butler, D. L., & Schnellert, L. (2012). Collaborative inquiry in teacher professional development. *Teaching and Teacher Education, 28*(8), 1206–1220.

Colton, A. B., Langer, G. M., & Goff, L. S. (2015). Create a safe space to learn. *The Learning Professional, 36*(3), 40.

Dunn, R. (2021). Teacher inquiry: Towards a typology of a teacher's inquiry disposition. *Professional Development in Education, 49*(5), 884–898.

Glickman, C., & Burns, R. W. (2020). *Leadership for learning: How to bring out the best in every teacher* (2nd ed.). ASCD.

Glickman, C. D., Gordon, S. P., Ross-Gordon, J. M., & Solis, R. D. (2024). *Supervision and instructional leadership: A developmental approach* (11th ed.). Pearson.

Gordon, S. P. (2008). Dialogic reflective inquiry: Integrative function of instructional supervision. *Catalyst for Change, 35*(2).

Gordon, S. P., & Solis, R. D. (2018). Teacher leaders of collaborative action research: Challenges and rewards. *Ie: Inquiry in Education, 10*(2), 3.

Hargreaves, A., & O'Connor, M. (2018). *Leading collaborative professionalism: Seminar series 274*. Centre for Strategic Education.

Hattie, J., & Smith, R. (2021). There's strength in empowering the collective. *Principal, 100*(3), 16–19.

Iraola, E. A., Romero, G. R., & Millera, M. J. (2024). Dialogue among educators: Rethinking and recreating scenarios of cooperative and inclusive learning. *International Journal of Educational Research Open, 6*, 100322.

Jarvis, J., Mila Lindhardt, E., Mthiyane, N. P., & Ruus, O. C. (2021). Empathetic-reflective-dialogical restorying as a teaching-learning strategy in teacher education. *Journal of Education for Teaching, 48*(3), 332–347.

King, P. M., & Kitchener, K. S. (2004). Reflective judgment: Theory and research on the development of epistemic assumptions through adulthood. *Educational Psychologist, 39*(1), 5–18.

Matre, S., & Solheim, R. (2016). Opening dialogic spaces: Teachers' metatalk on writing assessment. *International Journal of Educational Research, 80*, 188–203.

Messiou, K., & Ainscow, M. (2020). Inclusive inquiry: Student–teacher dialogue as a means of promoting inclusion in schools. *British Educational Research Journal, 46*(3), 670–687.

Miller, M. (2024). *Re-imagining professional development for social and emotional learning: A case study*. Doctoral dissertation. University of British Columbia.

Muhonen, H., Pakarinen, E., Rasku-Puttonen, H., & Lerkkanen, M. K. (2024). Educational dialogue and teacher occupational stress in relation to student math performance. *Scandinavian Journal of Educational Research, 68*(3), 539–557.

Nelson, T. H., Deuel, A., Slavit, D., & Kennedy, A. (2010). Leading deep conversations in collaborative inquiry groups. *The Clearing House, 83*(5), 175–179.

Nijhuis, A. J. G. (2021). *Reflective dialogue in professional learning communities for educational leaders.* Master's thesis. University of Twente.

Podolsky, A., Kini, T., & Darling-Hammond, L. (2019). Does teaching experience increase teacher effectiveness? A review of US research. *Journal of Professional Capital and Community, 4*(4), 286–308.

Ronfeldt, M., Farmer, S. O., McQueen, K., & Grissom, J. A. (2015). Teacher collaboration in instructional teams and student achievement. *American Educational Research Journal, 52*(3), 475–514.

Rusov, V. (2023). Reflective dialogue: A condition for the implementation of student-centered learning. *Buletinul științific al Universității de Stat, Bogdan Petriceicu Hasdeu, din Cahul, Seria, Stiinte Umanistice, 17*(1), 69–81.

Solis, R., & Gordon, S. P. (2019). Supervisor facilitation of action research: Fostering teacher inquiry. *Journal of Practitioner Research, 4*(2), 2.

Solis, R., & Gordon, S. P. (2020). Integrating multiple professional learning frameworks to assist teachers' reflective inquiry. *Ie: Inquiry in Education, 12*(1), 12.

Stewart, T. T., & Jansky, T. A. (2022). Novice teachers and embracing struggle: Dialogue and reflection in professional development. *Teaching and Teacher Education: Leadership and Professional Development, 1*, 100002.

Svendsen, B. (2020). Inquiries into teacher professional development—What matters? *Education, 140*(3), 111–130.

Twyford, K., Le Fevre, D., & Timperley, H. (2017). The influence of risk and uncertainty on teachers' responses to professional learning and development. *Journal of Professional Capital and Community, 2*(2), 86–100.

van Kruiningen, J. F. (2013). Educational design as conversation: A conversation analytical perspective on teacher dialogue. *Teaching and Teacher Education, 29*, 110–121.

Wallen, M., & Tormey, R. (2019). Developing teacher agency through dialogue. *Teaching and Teacher Education, 82*, 129–139.

Wilcoxen, C. L., Steiner, A. L., & Bell, J. (2022). Strengthening preservice teachers' understanding of culturally responsive classrooms through exposure, immersion, and dialogue. *Journal of Community Engagement and Scholarship, 14*(1).

Wilkinson, J. (2014). Collegial coaching conversations and action research as arenas for translating practices for school change. *Redress, 27*(1), 26–30.

CHAPTER 9

"LEARNING LOSS" AND OTHER MISGUIDED NARRATIVES FOR IMPEDING EDUCATIONAL CHANGE

Ira Bogotch
Florida Atlantic University, USA

Eleanor Su-Keene
Texas A&M University, USA

ABSTRACT

Chapter 9 by Professors Bogotch and Su-Keene challenges us to think deeply and critically about school-district change. Change, they argue, is ever-present and inevitable. Yet the tools and strategies we have utilized to affect meaningful change are neither sustained nor institutionalized as described in traditional change theories. Drawing upon the consequences of the COVID pandemic that led to "learning loss," they posit that an opportunity for real change was possible to thwart educational state and national imposed mandates for standardized testing and compliance to other innate measures. They draw upon transformational leadership literature to promote true emancipation, democracy, equity, and justice. The chapter contributors challenge readers to break through taken-for-granted notions of change by introducing the notions of narrative and disruptive leadership that, in the words of Maxine Greene, urges educators to "find an aperture in the wall of what is taken for granted; to pierce the webs of obscurity; to see and then to choose." Drs. Bogotch and Su-Keene end the chapter with a realistic case focusing on educational change beyond traditional conceptualizations of educational leadership. *Leading Change through Transformational School Leadership* thus ends with no easy solutions but much to consider.

Keywords: Progressive change; school district; institutional; educational change; education leaders; school equity and justice

---

Prefocus Guiding Questions

- What are your first responses to the following questions?
    1. Why does it seem like we are being asked to make changes every year?
        a. Are we supposed to embrace all change?
    2. Is it true, from your experiences in schools, that the only constant is change?
        a. If so, then why do you hear the following statements:
            i. If it isn't [ain't] broken, why fix it?
            ii. Let's not reinvent the wheel, people!
    3. Lastly, do you agree with Michael Fullan that "you can't mandate what matters?"

INTRODUCTION: CHANGE IS HAPPENING

Change is happening all around us, whether we notice it or not. The Wabanaki, a Native American confederacy of tribes, believes that "The past is present. Time ripples from a canoe as it moves through the water. These ripples are constant and present."[1] For Indigenous peoples worldwide, change is as natural as the wind, water, and earth. In contrast, Western social scientists have been wrestling with trying to understand change as it happens and, more pointedly, toward controlling change to better meet organizational and societal needs. Therefore, the difference is that for Indigenous peoples, change belongs to everyone; for social scientists, various change forces exist so that specific individuals can enhance social and educational opportunities for everyone.

Either change is there for everyone to promote/resist or, as in the social sciences, we identify individual change agents, for example, school leaders, as those with the power to intervene. Thus, researchers have asked what leaders should do when initiating change. What should leaders do to sustain change efforts? Such research questions identify the leader's role, positionality, capacities, and abilities, as well as a leader's moral duty to lead change. Not surprisingly, researchers then ask about the role of followers: why and under what conditions do followers accept or resist change?

From this logic, we conclude that the field of educational leadership, as a social science, looks to discover the sweet spot for a school leader to plan, design, and implement changes—ideally, with the support of others. In doing so, however, we have deliberately narrowed the possibilities for change.

In this chapter, we ask what-if questions. We seek to be disruptive and provocative. That means we avoid conventional wisdom on school leadership, change theories, and engage in thought experiments. We would begin by decoupling change from the exclusive concepts and behaviors of school leadership and school improvement and instead, look toward the ideas of change as being there and everywhere, whether as forces of good creating opportunities for growth and development or as instruments of control, delimiting change to specific ends, some better or worse than others.

In this manner, we begin to think of change similar to how the French philosopher-historian-linguist Michel Foucault reconceptualized the construct of power. Foucault rejected traditional views of power, meaning that instead of seeing power as coming from above or from a leader, which connotes a) a negative relationship with followers, b) an insistence on compliance with norms and rules, c) examples of prohibitions, censorship, and d) standardization/uniformity (McLaren, 2002, p. 37). Foucault posited that because power is relational,

> ... [I]t is omnipresent; it is constantly produced among and between persons, institutions, things, and groups of persons. Power is mobile, local, heterogenous, and unstable. Power comes from everywhere; it is exercised from innumerable points... Power is not possessed [by a leader]. (p. 37)

Might the same be said of educational change? It, too, is relational among members of an organization or community and, therefore, changes as relationships are ubiquitous. We can experience change through leadership behaviors and the narratives leaders and followers create as opportunities to direct and influence change. No particular individual or group fully possesses the power to make change, for change is everywhere, and we can choose to participate or, as is often the case, to resist. As such, we ask that you turn your attention to the different narratives that are communicated to motivate, captivate, or deceive leaders and followers seeking change.

Many school-related narratives unintentionally reproduce inequities repeatedly: think of the achievement gap (Ladson-Billings, 2006). Narratives that are repeated over and over again become realities. We believe, however, that there are narratives that promote new ideas, new relationships, and known and unknown possibilities. In thinking about change in this new way, we are not erasing school leadership, school improvement, or professional development as mechanisms for change. Rather, we are situating these activities (i.e., variables) within the many narratives of schooling that create the conditions/possibilities for change or, its opposite, resistance.

THE EVOLUTION OF CHANGE THEORY LITERATURE

How did we get here? Early theories on planned change (Bennis et al., 1961) argued that human interventions and planning could harness, under rational assumptions, the meanings and actions of change theory. However, following the writings of Michael Fullan and others, the educational meanings of change encompassed individual professional development, organizational development (i.e., relearning), and implementation processes. It brought the ideals of planned change into the world of schooling and school systems. Moreover, because the field of study now included educational structures and processes, the theoretical and practical questions revolved around how new ideas and innovations were best learned, developed, and institutionalized in schools and school systems. We should also credit Fullan for his insights that change is not only what happens on the outside to organizations but also becomes a central question of what educators think and feel.

In Fullan's many iterations, he moved toward visioning, moral purposes, and bottom-up and top-down leadership, always looking for the right levers, which he labeled change forces (Fullan, 2003). Unfortunately, both he and other change theorists grasped the ambitious social science notion of scaling up and building a generalizable change model. We say, unfortunately, because today, in 2024–25, no such model or comprehensive theory of change has yet to emerge. Instead, researchers using action research and organizational learning practices (Scharmer, 2016; Senge, 2006) have offered us different theories of action. To be clear, the shift in change thinking from comprehensive theories to theories of action was about making cumulative small gains that, when successful, could lead to larger, more significant gains. Ironically, change was still conceptualized inside learning processes and their implementation into practice, only this time; change was not as a model but rather a series of good tries or, as Dewey called it, supporting that which is good and educative (Taylor & Bogotch, 1993). For Dewey and Fullan, good actions were also defined as being moral.

In no way do the above paragraphs capture the full complexities of the different ideas on change theories. However, in our judgment, another category mistake was happening concurrently. That is, from the many empirical studies on school change, certain narratives derived from specific findings emerged only to be repeated by researchers again and again. Dewey (1971) referred to this phenomenon as "abiding frameworks"; others would call it conventional wisdom or common sense. We are calling it narratives or metanarratives. Every so often, an empirical study offered a finding that resonated with policymakers or other researchers for political, ideological, or moral reasons. These works were then cited repeatedly until they were assumed to be true beliefs. Rarely were any of these repeated truths subjected to rigorous experimental designs. Instead, using traditional surveys and interview protocols, the conclusions led to even more confirmation, not to innovation.

Researchers themselves cannot be held fully responsible for how their findings have been used or interpreted. Nevertheless, school leadership continued to be perceived as the major change force lever in research. The narratives surrounding change then emerged as a linear progression of school improvement. That is, the school leader (system or school) came upon a new idea that she/he/they believed would lead to an improvement over what had been before. With these two variables in place, school leadership and school improvement, the resulting findings looked for evidence to confirm (1) the role of leaders (and therefore their followers) and (2) whether or not school/classroom improvement followed. The problem, as we see it, and which tends to happen in educational research, is that once an idea or a narrative receives many citations, that idea becomes the right answer, or in this case, the truth statements about making change. Worse still, it is adopted and institutionalized as policy.

The School Leader and Messy Change

The legitimacy of educational leadership as a field is supported by a foundation that school leaders impact the education system and make changes. Indeed, schools across decades have demonstrated through various methodological approaches that good principals have a positive impact on student outcomes, learning environment, school climate, teachers' professional capacity, community relationships, and more (see Day et al., 2016; Grissom et al., 2021; Leithwood & Mascall, 2008; Robinson et al., 2008). While these effects are well-established in the literature, studies have also recorded the lived realities and messiness for principals who are continuously seeking positive change among a myriad of challenges, including inadequate funding, poor school infrastructure, heavy-handed accountability systems, and teacher and staff shortages. In turn, a principal's ability to create change is limited by external and internal factors, time, and personal factors.

Under these various challenges, principals often feel forced to make decisions daily where the choice is between bad or worse. In some of our more recent work, we found that principals in Florida were walking a tightrope as they navigated the politics of book bans and censorship (Su-Keene, 2022).

One principal had to weigh the consequences of removing books from her school library or leaving the principalship. Indeed, external and internal factors of the school force principals to make decisions that go against their own value system. DeMatthews and Mahwinney (2014) described the leadership challenges for two dedicated, though imperfect social justice principals. They argued that their schools' realities, history, and context made it a struggle to make decisions that benefit all special education students. In some instances, principals made difficult choices that went against their moral values. The researchers added,

> In reality, principals leading for social justice experience the physical, mental, and emotional ups and downs of the work, press on while engaging in ongoing battles inside and outside of the school, and learn new lessons based on past experiences" (p. 875).

Literature has also shown that principals' roles, responsibilities, and tasks have increased in recent decades (Mahfouz, 2020; Oplatka, 2017). Indeed, more than half of principals work an average of 60 hours a week (Taie & Lewis, 2023). Even though principals are working more, our recent work in this area suggests that the increased workload is a response to budget cuts and teacher/staff shortages. In essence, principals are picking up the responsibility of those they cannot recruit or do not have the funding to hire.

In a recent study, we shared how principals carried additional responsibilities of teachers, administrators, and staff they could not afford.

> Every year I [the principal] am doing more with less to get better results. We had to take away an administrator last year and that caused a lot of stress because I had to take on a whole number of responsibilities. (Su-Keene et al., 2024, p. 9)

Additionally, these immediate and short-term challenges make it difficult for principals to prioritize positive long-term change. Principals described how daily challenges usurped time and prevented their capacity to make important long-term decisions and plans that could support systemic changes in their schools. Another principal believed in developing students' curiosity and love for learning at her bilingual immersion school, but her school was chronically short teachers, meaning classes had to be split, and students moved to other classrooms on a daily basis. "I wasn't fully staffed with teachers until February so we were on a ragtag skeleton team." Since teacher absenteeism and leave were both constant and yet unpredictable, it required her immediate attention and action, taking time out of her day and making it difficult to focus on other tasks such as developing teachers' capacity.

There are many reasons why a new and different conception of educational change is warranted. The guiding questions in the pre-focus text box illustrate that changes are expected to happen frequently (or resisted!). The questions also tell us that change happens with lots of excess baggage. That is, it upsets certain routines that make people in their jobs/professions comfortable with the ordinary, the everyday. Change introduces uncertainty. As a result, making change is often unwelcome. That is, followers have not fully understood or accepted the change or reform imposed externally, often from a top-down hierarchical authority in a school or classroom.

It is not as if all school members, teachers, staff, or parents came together professionally and collaboratively and demanded that the change be made. And yet, the research literature on change as a theory of action calls for participation, collaboration, and even a series of good tries until the change has been sustained and culturally embraced. The literature speaks of learning and relearning, adjusting and adapting. How is it that the contradictions of our lived experiences in school systems and our realities are so out of line with published research? Moreover, why are school leaders charged with "leading" unwelcome changes?

If school members do not see the urgency, necessity, or increased efficacy of making change, what is the educational meaning of "leading" change? A school principal or headmaster is often the point person, the responsible party for initiating change. It is hard for us to imagine a single comprehensive theory of change that would not only outline a specific course of action but also convince others with different opinions to act uniformly in making changes. And yet, that is the change dilemma of a school leader (Sarid, 2019). Uncertainties surrounding change make school members uncomfortable with top-down imposed changes. What, then, should be a school leader's tacit change theory of action be?

A savvy school leader understands that all that has happened before influences how they and other school members think about change, either positively or negatively. A school leader's responses are often dictated by what has happened before. Therefore, unlike what John Kotter's (2012) best-selling text purports, change is neither linear nor encapsulated into fixed sequential steps to be followed literally. Instead, we believe that all school leaders need a repertoire of strategic theories of action alongside a willingness to engage with others in implementing changes. We further believe that change happens as a series of good tries from which both school leaders and school participants endeavor to teach and learn from one another to move forward. Thus, change, when it happens, zigs and zags. And, flexibility is probably a school leader's greatest strength when engaged in making changes.

Enter Transformational Approaches

In a personal communication, Tony Townsend talked about transformational leadership in two respects:

> ... the first relates to leadership that transforms education (currently known as "transformational leadership"); the second way is to consider how our understanding of educational leadership has changed (or transformed) over time and might do so further in the future. The first considers a specific form of educational leadership; the second enables us to look at a range of leadership approaches that have impacted educational (and particularly school) leadership.

In other words, there is no one sequence or checklist of specific leadership activities that guarantees or predicts how change will happen. Rather, we identify multiple theories of change, such as the evolution of distributive leadership (e.g., Gronn, Spillane), whereby concrete activities among school participants became central to change theory. For us, the only constant in all change theories is the need for learning and relearning, which has to extend beyond any one individual and become a collective response, ideally resulting in a professional and collaborative culture.

The overarching theme of transformational leadership was the need to build relationships with teachers to support their working together rather than simply managing and supervising what they did as individuals. What Leithwood (1992) meant by planning and problem-solving together has today become a matter of learning together, not individually, but collectively. Our case study below documents how individual and "organizational learning" continues to elude school practitioners, thus opening the door for policymakers to create misguided narratives that fit their political/ideological agendas. The case reveals how expert knowledge assigned to individuals promotes disparate educational objectives that are not conducive to working together, collaborating, or embracing changes. These expert narratives often come from above, externally, or from different disciplines, such as school psychology, special education, behavioral intervention, and managerialism.

In the USA, this is most evident inside the umbrella concept of accountability. At the beginning of the academic year, conversations with US school leaders note how laser-focused principals are on their schools' letter grades. This "letter-grade" narrative is built upon numerous metrics, each becoming school improvement priorities for the year. The narrative is on keeping the A in schools with a letter grade of A. In schools below A, the narrative is on raising the letter grade metric by metric. In so doing, many quality indicators fall outside the letter-grade narrative and are thus dismissed. Again, in our case example, we witness the dynamics of individual learning plans (IEPs 504s) and accommodations mandated by law, which may ironically contradict the individual student's educational needs. As educational specialists promote their expert power, the letter-grade narrative remains the proverbial elephant in the room. As a result, equitable change—meeting the needs of individual students—may not happen.

MISGUIDED NARRATIVES: "ACCOUNTABILITY," "LETTER-GRADES," AND "LEARNING LOSS" AS "PERSISTENT NARRATIVES OF PUBLIC EDUCATION FAILURE"

In this section, we will frame theories of change (e.g., transformational leadership, school improvement, etc.) within persistent historical and contemporary narratives of public education failure. Using an equity lens, we feel obligated to address outcome disparities correlated with socioeconomic status, race, and gender. Such correlations as repeated research findings have led educational leadership researchers to [unintentionally, we think] frame their social science research questions in deficit terms. Looking at contemporary US conditions for change, we read:

> ... the next conservative Administration should take sweeping action to assure that the purpose of the Civil Rights Act is not inverted through a disparate impact standard to provide a pretext for theoretically endless federal meddling. (Burke, 2024, p. 336)

The US political right associates disparate impacts with wrong-minded educational policies. The irony should not be lost on any of us: naming the problem of central governments meddling in local educational affairs, while trumpeting authoritarian mandates and dictates to the same local authorities. But what is also ironic is that typically it was liberal policymakers and researchers who defined educational reforms as objective, neutral, and a matter of social science that unintentionally blamed the victims—students of color, disabled, special education students, non-native speakers of English, LGBTQ students—for learning loss, the achievement gap, and low standardized test scores resulting in failing letter-grades. How far back has this deficit thinking occurred in the US?

An 1880 article titled, *The Public School Failure* by Richard Grant White (1880) could not have been any clearer. He asserted that public education was supposed to be for poor children only, but with governance and finance changes, public schools had been expanded to include all children and all grade levels. Thus, he asked, why wasn't public education a panacea for the economic, social, and political ills of society? Many Americans then and now would label public education a failure for not mitigating societal problems. White continued:

> ... however great may be the intrinsic value of education as a formative social agency, the effect of that which is afforded by our public-school system has proved in every way unsatisfactory and worse than unsatisfactory. (p. 538)

Drawing on student achievement data, White wrote:

> According to independent and competent evidence from all quarters, the mass of the pupils of these public schools are unable to read intelligently, to spell correctly, to write, legibly, to describe understandingly the geography of their own country, or to do anything that reasonable well-educated children should do with ease. (p. 541)

It is important to see how many weak empirical associations White was making. For example,

1. Claims of teacher deficiencies: calling teachers' limited knowledge "an embarrassment."
2. Associating public education with vice: it was a blight "upon morals, upon politics, and upon education" (p. 540), and
3. An engine of political corruption and social deterioration (p. 540)

White concluded that public schools were not helpful for the public good and, therefore, were a waste of taxpayer dollars. "The road to the best government of the people does not lie only through the door of the public schoolhouse." (p. 544)

The essay triggered a defense of public education which included articles in the New York Times ("The March Magazines. The North American Review," 1881)

> It is a libel, pure and simple, made up of an exaggerated statement of some of the poorest results contained in the report with some touches of false coloring. Mr. White's conclusions on the first count are, therefore, vitiated. His argument that the theory of public schools is false is a 'medley of fallacies'.

When we fast forward to March 2020, we witnessed schools worldwide shuttering their doors and moving to online learning almost overnight. Pandemic-induced schooling posed numerous challenges, including internet and technology inequities, limited teacher capacity for virtual learning, high student truancy, collective mental health struggles from isolation and stress, and food insecurity. Collectively, the effects prompted concerns about students' lack of learning during this extended timeframe. Nevertheless, research on pandemic-induced learning loss demonstrates mixed results. An early systematic review found that students performed lower on standardized tests in specific subjects like math, primary students had greater impacts than secondary students, and some studies found no evidence of learning loss (Donnelly & Patrinos, 2022). To date, the most cited article on pandemic-induced learning loss comes from a study in the Netherlands that demonstrates students lost three percentile points, equivalent to a fifth of a school year in their academic performance (Engzell et al., 2021). Another study modeled potential long-term learning loss from the pandemic and predicted that students would lose more than a year's learning from three-month closures and that with heavy remediation upon return, learning loss could be reduced by half a year (Kaffenberger, 2021). The infamous McKinsey's global study was framed as the "best case scenario" implicitly meaning that their results were much worse (Dorn et al., 2020). Why these dire conclusions?

What we see with misguided narratives from accountability, letter grades, achievement gap, vulnerable populations, and hence, learning loss is the predictable (desirable?) failure of public education. Proponents of these narratives had a larger mission in mind; quite literally, they went after the public funding of public education, concluding that privatization of education works better (e.g., voucher systems, charter schools, even homeschooling).

Thus, public education is no stranger to systemic attacks from both sides of the political aisle. Policymakers have agendas to win popular support. They need a message: failure, mismanagement, and waste. Fortunately, researchers have looked for counternarratives that redefine the real losses among children and adults as social, mental, and physical. Yet, these counternarratives have not replaced the policies and practices of standardized tests and accountability measures. As critical researchers, we would argue that the "learning loss" rhetoric is a neoliberal strategy that capitalizes on a crisis. Like its historical rhetorical counterparts—at-risk students, achievement gap, and No Child Left Behind—learning loss narratives have stymied schools' capacity to change, to do better for children especially those from marginalized backgrounds (Ladson-Billings, 2021). Instead, educational policymakers double-down on rote, mechanistic learning for the sake of higher test scores. Loewenberg Ball (2024) cautions

> It should worry us that, as a nation, the United States seems to be invested in tearing down the enormous possibility and promise of public education. In retelling that our children's opportunities have been irredeemably destroyed, we impair the possibility of collective inspiration for how to move forward. Instead of seeing and building on children's cultural and intellectual capacities, we are stuck in a swamp of behindness that creates an urgency of "catching up." This swamp spawns policy initiatives that seek to control and punish rather than contribute to and develop.

It follows, therefore, that:

The 'achievement gap,' then, isn't inevitable. It's baked into the system, resulting from the decisions adults make, consciously and unconsciously, about which students get what resources. It's a gap of our own design. ("The Opportunity Myth", 2018)

CONCLUSION: NARRATIVE AND DISRUPTIVE LEADERSHIP POSSIBILITIES IN SCHOOLS

We conclude that educational leadership research needs to reconceptualize both leadership and change. We are seeing the emergence of new frameworks including disruptive leadership, narrative change, and humanizing leadership across fields (Brennan, 2022; Haapanen et al., 2024; Su-Keene, 2022). Themes emerging from these frameworks including challenging existing structures, power, and status quo; valuing the humanity of individuals; reframing mental models to prioritize assets over deficits; and a shift from fixing to re-inventing. Practically, the first steps for education is to offer existing counternarratives to replace failure, deficit thinking, and learning loss. While these negative narratives have been circulated and perpetuated by politicians, media, researchers, etc., few have explored the narratives of those who are on the crossroads of these realities: teachers. In an unlikely platform, the non-profit company, Donors Choose, surveyed over 1,000 teachers to explore students' outcomes because of the pandemic (Redefining "Learning Loss", 2021). Teachers shared the following:

- Impact learning: "Learning loss implies that kids have lost the ability to learn or that learning has not occurred. Learning takes so many forms and occurs in so many ways it's unfair to say students have learning loss because they were not physically in a school building."—Leslie, New Jersey
- Digital learning: "There is no learning loss. Our children just focus on a different set of skills—mainly life skills—and learn to adapt to a different style of learning (mostly digital)."—Katie, Massachusetts
- Pandemic disconnection: "We shouldn't approach this year with a deficit mindset but rather what our students have gained. They've learned technology skills that will benefit them in their future. Many have learned more life skills. There was a great deal of learning last year, just maybe not with the standard curriculum."—Becky, Massachusetts
- Nothing—the term shouldn't exist at all! "Our educational system is so focused on outdated scheduling and materials that were intended back during the Industrial Revolution, rather than skills and subjects that would benefit today's technological-based society. While students as a whole may not know the same things the previous generations knew, how many times has someone said 'I didn't need _____ in my adult life'?"—Shaylyn, California

Taking a cue from successful, experienced workers, we might contrast the pros and cons of the "school of hard knocks" to "book learning." Here, the latter term is viewed as being deficient, turning student achievement on its head. What about attributing what students learned over the summer, during the pandemic, or during absenteeism as real-world experiences? Learning takes on many more forms and occurs in many ways besides formal instruction and test results. While out of school, children and young adults are engaged in learning different sets of skills, many useful for life. And while the current policy environment has opposed social media, our students have become so skilled and talented in these digital environments. True, educators need to guide the lessons to be learned and applied, but in no way is this learning loss. A more accurate description to replace learning loss would be to acknowledge the changes in generational knowledge and skills. School is literally "old school" learning and not total learning of lifelong experiences.

CASE STUDY

Educational Change for Ruth: A Mother's Intuition and Advocacy

Here, we hope to add to our conceptual argument with an empirical case about an eight-year-old named Ruth and the educational change and advocacy from her mother's/Jane's perspective. We focus on Ruth and Jane's story to provide a counternarrative to post-pandemic educational "normality."

Like many children of her age, Ruth was excited about starting Kindergarten at a new school in the fall of 2020. Instead, Ruth's summer blended anti-climactically into the school year when she got out of bed one morning and sat at the dining table on a school-loaned chrome book to meet her teacher and classmates for the first time. Ruth was initially excited and got through the first six-hour school days with little difficulty. However, by the third day, the combination of low engagement, her attention deficit hyperactivity disorder (ADHD), and lack of differentiated learning to meet her academic needs made it difficult for her to focus, stay in one place, or learn meaningfully.

To make matters worse, two months after the virtual roll-out, students were allowed to return to school or remain online, resulting in a hybrid format. As her teacher attended to the challenges of managing two classrooms—one in person and the other online—far less attention was given to the three remaining students in the virtual classroom. Recognizing these challenges, Jane said that the teacher was flexible with students online and allowed Ruth to read, which she loved, anytime Ruth felt restless or bored if she could demonstrate her understanding of the assignment on hand.

In the following year, Jane decided to homeschool Ruth for the first half of first grade so that Ruth could be vaccinated before attending in-person schooling. Ruth had no formal instruction but rather spent her days reading. By this point, Ruth had learned about genres and developed preferences for the types of books she enjoyed most. The rest of the time was spent playing outdoors and playing games. When Ruth returned to public school, the transition was smoother than Jane anticipated. She quickly made friends, adjusted to a schedule, and was at or above grade level in math and reading, which surprised her teachers when informed about her recent educational background. In addition to the general education classroom, Ruth—who was diagnosed as twice exceptional—was provided with two support systems: a 504 plan for her ADHD and participation in a pull-out, gifted and talented program.

Despite the alternative educational formats, Ruth's educational experience leading up to in-person public education was rather idyllic. Unfortunately, challenges for Ruth began upon her full entry into the public school system. Although Ruth was academically above grade level, Ruth's ADHD impacted her awareness of social cues, working memory, and emotional regulation which created the perception for her teachers that her behavioral actions were intentional. For the past few years, Ruth has had experienced veteran teachers who had nonetheless adopted post-COVID narratives around student behavior. That is, student behavior was worse than pre-COVID schooling. Jane documented the teachers' concerns about Ruth's education for the past two years through email correspondences and 504 meetings. Jane provided us with the teachers' concerns documented below:

1. Ruth had an extra hard time staying focused long enough to get her math work finished this afternoon. She needed many more reminders than usual.
2. She was very talkative in Mrs. X's room this morning. I was told that at lunch she was throwing her lunchbox around. She had many reminders and still struggled with her self-control.
3. We are concerned about her growth, even though she's in the 99th percentile, we should still be seeing growth.
4. It sounds like you want us to treat her differently, but all kids deserve to be treated fairly.
5. We believe there still needs to be consequences for bad behavior.

When Ruth was asked about her experience in school, she was apathetic and said:

1. The teachers yell at me every day. I think me, and maybe another kid, get yelled at the most.
2. I don't like school because I get recess taken away. I want to be homeschooled again.
3. I don't want to go to school because my teachers don't like me, but I don't want to move classrooms or schools because I want to be with my friends.
4. I don't learn much in school, but gifted and talented is fun because we get to do fun projects.
5. I like art, music, and computer classes.

In trying to address some of the teachers' and Ruth's concerns, Jane met with the teachers, counselors, and administrative team on various occasions to find ways to support Ruth's needs. In several attempts, Jane tried to re-frame Ruth's behavior for the teachers. In a recent 504 meeting, she said,

> I tried to put Ruth's behavior in a way they could understand. Kids come into the class at all different reading levels, right? And teachers meet the kids where they are and build them up. I tried to get the teachers to see this with behavior as something similar in skill. Kids are at different development abilities for controlling emotions and impulses so we need to meet them where they are and work with them. Would we ever punish a child who was struggling to read by taking away their recess?

Additionally, Jane pushed back against traditional accommodations that she was provided on the 504 plan. She said,

> The school gave me a template where there was a list of accommodations like preferential seating and extra time on tests with checkmark boxes next to them. Not only did these accommodations not meet Ruth's actual needs, but how dehumanizing it felt to go off a grocery list of random technical things.

Instead, Jane asked for the teachers to create an atmosphere where Ruth could have "a positive elementary experience where she felt loved and cared for." When Jane felt that the 504 meetings became insufficient, she began to meet with the administrative team to share her concerns. In a meeting with the principal, Jane emphasized their family's hopes and dreams for Ruth. She said, "After the pandemic, we knew that the most important thing was that our children were healthy, happy, and had the capacity to live a meaningful life."

The principal was empathetic to Jane's concerns and Ruth's classroom experiences. She and the assistant principal said that they would have conversations with the teachers to be more positive with children in the classroom and to be proactive with Ruth's behavior. The principal assured Jane that the school centered around the whole child and that she would find ways to attend to Ruth's needs. The principal also offered to move Ruth to a different set of teachers, but Jane was conflicted, "Ruth had great friendships which we felt should be prioritized. We can't advocate for her to have friends, but we can advocate for her needs with her teachers" and decided to keep her with her original teachers.

After a year and a half with little positive change, Jane noticed that the school environment was taking a toll on Ruth's self-esteem and well-being. During that time, she stayed in touch with the principal, who had recently lost a parent to cancer, and with only half a year left, Jane decided to be proactive in supporting Ruth on her own. Being a working mother, it was not feasible for Ruth to go back to homeschooling. However, Jane made arrangements with the school to take Ruth out of school for ADHD coaching appointments and doctor appointments. On several occasions, Ruth's parents took her on work trips where she was allowed to make up missed assignments and provide some documentation of an educational experience. While

Jane did not explicitly lay out her intent with the administration, Jane's plan was to try to remove Ruth from as much in-person schooling as possible and minimize the emotional harm that she felt Ruth was experiencing. She said,

> I get it. The teachers have a lot going on. They have a lot of students. They're overworked, underpaid, and underappreciated. The principal is supportive and tries as much as she can, but she's also overworked because they're understaffed, and now, she's grieving her mother. Ironically, I feel like the best education she can have right now is to be out of that classroom, and I just hope that next year will be different.

In the US, chronic absences and truancy are major concerns for schools. After the pandemic, truancy was a big concern because schools did not know students' whereabouts and are not able to get in contact with parents. In the state where Ruth attends school, funding is based on attendance rather than enrollment which means Ruth's absences would negatively impact the school. While Jane was frustrated about Ruth's situation, she did not wish to negatively impact the school as a whole, so she found ways to strategically navigate this dilemma. She scheduled Ruth's appointments shortly after attendance was taken in the late morning. She was also in communication with the teachers and administration about travel and educational trips. For the rest of the school year, Jane helped Ruth maintain her academic requirements and friendships in school, but also found alternatives environments to mitigate emotional harm that Ruth was experiencing in a post-pandemic schooling reality around compliance and behavior.

REFLECTIONS ON THE CASE

We provide the case of Ruth's educational experience and Jane's advocacy as an example of educational change beyond traditional conceptualizations of educational leadership. Here, the parent is acting as the change agent within her capacity to support her daughter's educational experience within the broader narratives of US public education. In this case, we demonstrate that educational change is a series of good tries, compromises, and good intentions that aim for more positive benefits than negative harm. This is a case grounded in pragmatism, that is, a process of human actions that are taken to re-adapt to an environment and continuously assessed to determine change (Dewey, 1971). As researchers, we argue for a re-invention of educational change and educational leadership that can lead to action, learning, and, thereby, change.

We encourage the readers to consider the following points for discussion:

- In what ways can non-educational stakeholders (e.g., parents, community, businesses) support educational change away from "learning loss" narratives? Moreover, would it resonate?
- In what ways are there tensions between educators' and leaders' workload and the ability to create change?

- Single case research has been instrumental in fields like medicine, psychology, and behavioral science (e.g., first vaccine by Edward Jenner tested on James Phillip in 1796, Pavlov's studies on classical conditioning, B.F. Skinner's theory of behavioralism). What role can single-case research play in developing theories of educational change?

NOTE

1. Jamie Bissonette Lewey, member of the Abenaki tribe.

REFERENCES

Bennis, W. G., Benne, K. D., & Chin, R. (Eds.). (1961). *The planning of change: Readings in the applied behavioral sciences.* Holt, Rinehart & Winston.

Brennan, N. B. (2022). Disruptive leadership: Making waves, thriving when it is hard to be a leader. *Nurse Leader, 20*(1), 52–55.

Burke, L. (2024). Department of education. In P. Dans & S. Groves (Eds.), *Mandate for leadership: The conservative promise.* Heritage Foundation. https://static.project2025.org/2025_MandateForLeadership_FULL.pdf

Day, C., Gu, Q., & Sammons, P. (2016). The impact of leadership on student outcomes: How successful school leaders use transformational and instructional strategies to make a difference. *Educational Administration Quarterly, 52*(2), 221–258.

DeMatthews, D., & Mawhinney, H. (2014). Social justice leadership and inclusion: Exploring challenges in an urban district struggling to address inequities. *Educational Administration Quarterly, 50*(5), 844–881.

Dewey, J. (1971). *Reconstruction in philosophy* (No. 48). Beacon Press.

Donnelly, R., & Patrinos, H. A. (2022). Learning loss during Covid-19: An early systematic review. *Prospects, 51*(4), 601–609.

Dorn, E., Hancock, B., Sarakatsannis, J., & Viruleg, E. (December, 2020). *COVID-19 and learning loss—Disparities grow and students need help* (Vol. 8, pp. 6–7). McKinsey & Company.

Engzell, P., Frey, A., & Verhagen, M. D. (2021). Learning loss due to school closures during the COVID-19 pandemic. *Proceedings of the National Academy of Sciences, 118*(17).

Fullan, M. (2003). *Change forces with a vengeance.* Routledge.

Grissom, J. A., Egalite, A. J., & Lindsay, C. A. (2021). How principals affect students and schools. *Wallace Foundation, 2*(1), 30–41.

Haapanen, K. A., Christens, B. D., Speer, P. W., & Freeman, H. E. (2024). Narrative change for health equity in grassroots community organizing: A study of initiatives in Michigan and Ohio. *American Journal of Community Psychology, 73*(3–4), 390–407.

Kaffenberger, M. (2021). Modelling the long-run learning impact of the Covid-19 learning shock: Actions to (more than) mitigate loss. *International Journal of Educational Development, 81,* 102326.

Kotter, J. P. (2012). *Leading change.* Harvard Business Review Press.

Ladson-Billings, G. (2006). From the achievement gap to the education debt: Understanding achievement in US schools. *Educational Researcher, 35*(7), 3–12.

Ladson-Billings, G. (2021). I'm here for the hard re-set: Post pandemic pedagogy to preserve our culture. *Equity & Excellence in Education, 54*(1), 68–78.

Leithwood, K. (1992). The move toward transformational leadership. *Educational Leadership, 49,* 8–12.

Leithwood, K., & Mascall, B. (2008). Collective leadership effects on student achievement. *Educational Administration Quarterly, 44*(4), 529–561.

Loewenberg Ball, D. (2024, February 16). Why is the nation invested in tearing down public education? *Education Week.* https://www.edweek.org/teaching-learning/opinion-why-is-the-nation-invested-in-tearing-down-public-education/2024/02

Mahfouz, J. (2020). Principals and stress: Few coping strategies for abundant stressors. *Educational Management Administration & Leadership, 48*(3), 440–458.

McLaren, M. A. (2002). *Feminism, Foucault, and embodied subjectivity.* SUNY Press.

Oplatka, I. (2017). Principal workload: Components, determinants and coping strategies in an era of standardization and accountability. *Journal of Educational Administration, 55*(5), 552–568.

Redefining "Learning Loss". (2021, August 26). The DonorsChoose Blog. https://blog.donorschoose.org/articles/rethininking-learning-loss

Robinson, V. M., Lloyd, C. A., & Rowe, K. J. (2008). The impact of leadership on student outcomes: An analysis of the differential effects of leadership types. *Educational Administration Quarterly, 44*(5), 635–674.

Sarid, A. (2019). Social justice dilemmas: A multidimensional framework of social justice educational leadership. *Leadership and Policy in Schools, 20*(2), 149–167. https://doi.org/10.1080/15700763.2019.1631856

Scharmer, C. O. (2016). *Theory U: Leading from the future as it emerges.* Berrett-Koehler Publishers.

Senge, P. M. (2006). *The fifth discipline: The art and practice of the learning organization.* Broadway Business.

Su-Keene, E. (2022). *Under pressure: Exploring school leadership changes Pre-COVID-19 and post George Floyd using an abductive approach* Doctoral dissertation. Florida Atlantic University..

Su-Keene, E. J., DeMatthews, D. E., & Keene, A. C. (2024). Principal work stress and its relationship with mental health, sleep quality, and leadership self-efficacy: An exploratory mixed-methods approach. *Leadership and Policy in Schools,* 1–19.

Taie, S., & Lewis, L. (2023). *Principal attrition and mobility: Results from the 2021–22 principal follow-up survey to the national teacher and principal survey. First look.* NCES 2023-046. National Center for Education Statistics..

Taylor, D. L., & Bogotch, I. E. (1993, January 28). *Teacher working conditions and school reform: A descriptive analysis* [Paper presentation]. Southwest Educational Research Association..

The March Magazines. (1881, February 19). The North American review. *New York Times.* https://timesmachine.nytimes.com/timesmachine/1881/02/19/103399961.pdf?pdf_redirect=true&ip=0

TNTP. (2018). *The opportunity myth: What students can show us about how school is letting them down—And how to fix it.* https://tntp.org/tntp_the-opportunity-myth_web/

White, R. (1880). The public-school failure. *North American Review, 131*(289), 537–550. http://www.jstor.org/stable/25100917ß

www.ingramcontent.com/pod-product-compliance
Lightning Source LLC
Chambersburg PA
CBHW050537300426
44113CB00012B/2152